FRENCH
PHRASEBOOK

GEDDES&
GROSSET

© 1998 Geddes & Grosset Ltd, David Dale House,
New Lanark, ML11 9DJ

ISBN 1 85534 340 1

Printed and bound in France by Maury Eurolivres

2 4 6 8 10 9 7 5 3 1

CONTENTS

CONTENTS

CONTENTS

KEY TO PRONUNCIATION

Guide to French pronunciation scheme

ah	as in b<u>a</u>d, f<u>a</u>r, f<u>a</u>ther
ai	as in m<u>e</u>t, <u>e</u>xcuse, w<u>e</u>ll, m<u>e</u>rcy
ay	as in ob<u>ey</u>, d<u>a</u>y
aw	as in h<u>o</u>t, bl<u>o</u>t, f<u>ough</u>t
ee	as in m<u>ea</u>l, f<u>ee</u>l, souven<u>i</u>r
er	as in th<u>e</u>, t<u>i</u>ck, speak<u>er</u>
ew	as in b<u>eau</u>tiful*
oo	as in tr<u>u</u>e, bl<u>u</u>e, gl<u>ue</u>
oh	as in n<u>o</u>te, b<u>oa</u>t

* There is no exact equivalent in English for the French 'closed' oo sound. Try with your lips to make the oo shape, while saying the ee sound through them.

The other area of French pronunciation without exact equivalents in English is the ng sounds, reduced here for simplicity to two:

an	as in French compr<u>end</u> (sounds like ong, as in s<u>ong</u>)
ern	as in French b<u>ien</u> (sounds like ang, as in b<u>ang</u>)

French consonants are pronounced much as in English.

GETTING STARTED

Everyday words and phrases

Yes
Oui
wee

No
Non
non

Please
S'il vous plaît
seel voo play

Yes, please
Oui, s'il vous plaît
wee, seel voo play

No, thank you
Non, merci
non, mair-see

Thank you
Merci
mair-see

Good
Bien
byern

OK
Ça va
sah vah

Excuse me
Excusez-moi
aiks-kew-say-mwah

I am very sorry
Je suis désolé
jer swee day-soh-lay

Being understood

I do not understand
Je ne comprends pas
jer ner kohm-pran pah

I understand
Je comprends
jer kohm-pran

Do you understand?
Comprenez-vous?
kohm-prer-nay-voo?

I do not speak French
Je ne parle pas français
jer ner pahrl pah fran-say

Do you speak English?
Parlez-vous anglais?
par-lay-voo zan-glay

Can you help me, please?
Pouvez-vous m'aider, s'il vous plaît?
poo-vay-voo may-day, seel voo play

Could you repeat that?
Pourriez-vous répétez, s'il vous plaît?
poo-ryay-voo ray-pay-tay, seel voo play

Please repeat that slowly
Répétez lentement, s'il vous plaît
ray-pay-tay lan-ter-man, seel voo play

Please write it down
Notez-le, s'il vous plaît
noh-tay-ler, seel voo play

Can you translate this for me?
Pouvez-vous me traduire ceci?
poo-vay-voo me trah-dweer ser-see

Is there someone who speaks English?
Y a-t-il quelqu'un qui parle anglais?
ee-ah-teel kail-kern kee pahrl an-glay

Please point to the phrase in the book
Montrez-moi la phrase dans le livre, s'il vous plaît
mon-tray mwah la frahz dan ler leevr, seel voo play

It does not matter
Ce n'est rien
ser nai ryern

I do not mind
Ça ne me dérange pas
sa ner mer day-ranj pah

Greetings and exchanges

Hello
Bonjour
bon-joor

Hi
Salut
sah-lew

Good morning
Bonjour
bon-joor

Good evening
Bonsoir
bon-swahr

How are you?
Comment allez-vous?
koh-man tah-lay voo

I am very well, thank you
Très bien, merci
trai byern, mair-see

It is good to see you
Je suis heureux de vous voir
jer swee zer-rer der voo vwahr

It is nice to meet you
Heureux de faire votre connaissance
her-rer der fair vohtr koh-nay-sans

That is very kind of you
Vous êtes très aimable
voo zait trai zai-mahbl

You are very kind
Vous êtes bien aimable
voo zait byern ay-mahbl

You are very welcome
Je vous en prie
jer voo zan pree

Good night
Bonne nuit
bohner nwee

Goodbye
Au revoir
oh rer-vwahr

Greetings and exchanges

See you soon
A bientôt
ah byern-toh

My name is...
Je m'appelle...
jer mah-pail

What is your name?
Comment vous appelez-vous?
koh-man voo zah-play voo

Here is my son
Voici mon fils
vwah-see mon fees

This is — my daughter
Voici — ma fille
vwah-see — mah fee

I am from — Britain
Je suis — Britannique
jer swee — bree-tah-neek

— England
— Anglais
— ang-lay

— Scotland
— Ecossais
— zay-koh-say

This is — my husband
Voici — mon mari
vwah-see — mon mah-ree

— my wife
— ma femme
— mah fahm

I am on holiday
Je suis en vacances
jer swee zan vah-kans

I am a student
Je suis étudiant
jer swee zay-tew-dyan

I live in London
J'habite à Londres
jah-beet ah londr

Common questions

I am from — Wales
Je suis — Gallois
jer swee — gahl-wah

> **— Ireland**
> — Irlandais
> *— zeer-lan-day*

> **— America**
> — Américain
> *— zah-may-reek-ern*

> **— Australia**
> — Australien
> *— zoh-strah-lyern*

> **— South Africa**
> — Sud-Africain
> *— sewd-ahf-ree-kern*

> **— New Zealand**
> — Néo-Zélandais
> *— nayoh-zay-lan-day*

Common questions

Where?
Où?
oo

Where is...?
Où se trouve...?
oo ser troov...

Common questions

Where are...?
Où se trouvent...?
oo ser troov...

How much?
Combien?
kohm-byern

When?
Quand?
kan

Who?
Qui?
kee

What?
Quoi/Comment?
kwah/koh-mon

Why?
Pourquoi?
poor-kwah

How?
Comment?
koh-man

Which?
Lequel?
ler-kail

Have you got any change?
Avez-vous de la monnaie?
ahvay voo der lah moh-nay

How long will it take?
Il y en a pour combien de temps?
eel-yohn-ah poor kohm-byern der tan

How much do I have to pay?
Combien dois-je payer?
kohm-byern dwah-jer pay-yay

What do you call this in French?
Comment appelez-vous ceci en français?
koh-man tah-play voo ser-see an fran-say

Common questions

What does this mean?
Que veut dire ceci?
ker ver deer ser-see

What is the problem?
Quel est le problème?
kail ai ler proh-blaim

What is this?
Qu'est-ce que c'est?
kais-ker say

Who did this?
Qui a fait cela?
kee ah fay ser-lah

What is wrong?
Qu'est-ce qui ne va pas?
kais-kee ner vah pah

What time do you close?
A quelle heure fermez-vous?
ah kail err fair-may voo

Where can I change my clothes?
Où puis-je me changer?
oo pwee-jer mer shan-gay

Who should I see about this?
A qui puis-je m'adresser?
ah kee pwee-jer mah-drai-say

Where can I buy a postcard?
Où puis-je acheter une carte postale?
oo pwee-jer ahsh-tay ewn kahrt pohs-tahl

How can I contact American Express/Diners Club?
Comment puis-je contacter American Express/Diners Club?
koh-man pwee-jer kon-tahk-tay ah-may-ree-kan aik-sprais/dee-nairs kloob

Do you know a good restaurant?
Connaissez-vous un bon restaurant?
koh-nai-say voo zern bon rais-toh-ran

Do you mind if I...?
Est-ce que ça vous dérange si...?
ais-ker sah voo day-ranj see...

May I borrow your map?
Puis-je emprunter votre plan?
pwee-jer an-prern-tay vohtr plan

Asking the time

What time is it?
Quelle heure est-il?
kail err ay-teel

It is...
Il est...
eel ai

a quarter past ten
dix heures et quart
dee-zerr ay kahr

a quarter to eleven
onze heures moins le quart
on-zerr mwan ler kahr

after three o'clock
après trois heures
ah-prai trwah zerr

at about one o'clock
vers une heure
vair ewn err

at half past six
à six heures et demie
ah see-zerr ay der-mee

at night
la nuit
lah nwee

before midnight
avant minuit
ah-van mee-nwee

early
de bonne heure
der bohn err

Asking the time

eleven o'clock
onze heures
onz err

midnight
minuit
mee-nwee

five past ten
dix heures cinq
deez err sank

nearly five o'clock
presque cinq heures
praisk sank err

five to eleven
onze heures moins cinq
onz err mwan sank

soon
bientôt
byern-toh

half past eight exactly
huit heures et demie pile
weet err zai der-mee peel

ten o'clock
dix heures
dee zerr

half past ten
dix heures et demie
deez err zai der-mee

ten past ten
dix heures dix
dee zerr dees

in an hour's time
dans une heure
dan zewn err

ten to eleven
onze heures moins dix
on zerr mwan dees

in half an hour
dans une demi-heure
dan zewn der-mee err

this afternoon
cet après-midi
sait ah-prai mee-dee

late
tard
tahr

this evening
ce soir
ser swahr

this morning
ce matin
ser mahtern

tonight
cette nuit
sait nwee

twelve o'clock (midday)
midi
mee-dee

twenty-five past ten
dix heures vingt-cinq
dee zerr vern-sank

twenty to eleven
onze heures moins vingt
onz err mwan vern

two hours ago
il y a deux heures
eel ee ah derr zerr

Common problems

I have no currency
Je n'ai pas d'argent liquide
jer nay pah dahr-jan lee-keed

I have dropped a contact lens
J'ai laissé tomber une lentille
jay lay-say tohm-bay ewn lan-tee

I cannot find my driving licence
Je ne trouve pas mon permis de conduire
jer ner troov pah mon pair-mee der kon-dweer

I have lost my credit cards
J'ai perdu mes cartes de crédit
jay pair-dew may kahrt der kray-dee

Common problems

I must see a lawyer
Je veux voir un avocat
jer ver vwahr ern ah-voh-kah

My car has been stolen
On m'a volé ma voiture
on mah voh-lay mah vwah-tewr

My handbag has been stolen
On m'a volé mon sac
on mah voh-lay mon sahk

My wallet has been stolen
On m'a volé mon portefeuille
on mah voh-lay mon pohrt-fery

AT THE AIRPORT

The main airport in Paris is Charles de Gaulle, though some flights use the other airport at Orly. There are regular rail and coach services linking Paris to both airports. You can fly to Paris from various UK provincial airports, as well as from Heathrow and Gatwick. Other places you can fly to from the UK include Biarritz, Bordeaux, Clermont-Ferrand, Lyon, Marseille and Toulouse.

Buses connecting Charles de Gaulle Airport to the centre of Paris are regular and reasonably priced, although in heavy traffic the journey may take up to an hour (bear this in mind if you decide to take a taxi). Using the *RER* (suburban express train) is a quicker option and is also reasonably priced: departing from Roissy *TGV* station, or Gare du Nord and Châtelet where you can transfer to the Métro.

The airport at Orly also has a regular bus service to the centre and bus links to local train stations.

Arrival

Here is my passport
Voici mon passeport
vwah-see mon pahs-pohr

Arrival

We have a joint passport
Nous avons un passeport conjoint
noo zah-von ern pahs-pohr kon-jwern

I am attending a convention
Je participe à une convention
jer pahr-tee-seep ah ewn con-van-syon

I am here on business
Je suis ici pour affaires
jer swee zee-see poor ahf-air

I will be staying here for eight weeks
Je reste huit semaines
jer raist wee ser-main

We are visiting friends
Nous sommes chez des amis
noo sohm shay day-zah-mee

I have nothing to declare
Je n'ai rien à déclarer
jer nay ryern ah day-klah-ray

I have the usual allowances
J'ai les quantités permises
jay lay kan-tee-tay pair-meez

This is for my own use
C'est pour mon usage personnel
sai poor mon ew-sahj pair-soh-nail

Common problems and requests

I have lost my ticket
J'ai perdu mon billet
jay pair-dew mon bee-yay

I have lost my traveller's cheques
J'ai perdu mes chèques de voyage
jay pair-dew may shaik der vohy-ahj

I have missed my connection
J'ai raté ma correspondance
jay rah-tay mah koh-rais-pon-dans

The people who were to meet me have not arrived
Les gens qui devaient venir me chercher ne sont pas arrivés
*lay jan kee der-vay ver-neer mer shair-shay ner son pah
zah-ree-vay*

I am in a hurry
Je suis pressé
jer swee prai-say

I am late
Je suis en retard
jer swee zan rer-tahr

Where will I find the airline representative?
Où puis-je trouver l'agent de la compagnie aérienne?
oo pwee-jer troovai lah-jan der lah kon-pah-nee ai-ree-ain

Common problems and requests

I have lost my bag
J'ai perdu mon sac
jay pair-dew mon sahk

Where can I buy currency?
Où puis-je changer de l'argent?
oo pwee-jer shan-jay der lahr-jan

Where can I change traveller's cheques?
Où puis-je changer des chèques de voyage?
oo pwee-jer shan-jay day shaik der vohy-ahj

Where is — the bar?
Où est — le bar?
oo ai — ler bahr

— the lounge?
— le salon d'attente?
— ler sah-lon dah-tant

— the transfer desk?
— le guichet de transit?
— ler gee-shay der tran-see

— the information desk?
— le bureau de renseignements?
— ler bew-roh der ran-sain-yer-man

— the toilet?
Où sont — les toilettes?
oo son — lay twah-lait

Is there a bus into town?
Y a-t-il un autobus pour aller en ville?
ee-ah-teel ern oh-toh-bews poor ah-lay an veel

Can I upgrade to first class?
Puis-je prendre un billet de première classe?
pwee-jer prandr ern bee-yay der prer-mee-air klahs

Where do I get the connection flight to Nice?
Où dois-je prendre la correspondance pour Nice?
oo dwah-jer prandr lah koh-rais-pon-dans poor nees

Luggage

Where is the baggage from flight number...?
Où sont les bagages du vol numéro...?
oo son lay bah-gahj dew vohl new-may-roh...

My luggage has not arrived
Mes valises ne sont pas arrivées
may vah-leez ner son pah zah-ree-vay

Where is my bag?
Où est mon sac?
oo ai mon sahk

It is — a large suitcase
C'est — une grande valise
sai — tewn grand vah-leez

Luggage

It is — a rucksack
C'est — un sac à dos
sai — tern sahk ah doh

— a small case
— une petite valise
— tewn per-teet vah-leez

These bags are not mine
Ces sacs ne sont pas à moi
say sahk ner son pah ah mwah

Where do I pick up my bags?
Où reprend-on ses bagages?
oo rer-pran-ton say bah-gahj

Are there any luggage trolleys?
Y a-t-il des chariots à bagages?
ee-ah-teel day shah-ryoh ah bah-gahj

Can I check in my bags?
Puis-je enregistrer mes bagages?
pwee-jan-ray-jees-tray may bah-gahj

Can I have help with my bag?
Y a-t-il un porteur?
ee-ah-teel ern pohr-terr

Careful, the handle is broken
Attention, la poignée est cassée
ah-tan-syon, lah pwah-nyay ai kah-say

This package is fragile
Ce paquet est fragile
ser pah-kay ai frah-jeel

I will carry that myself
Je porterai ceci moi-même
jer pohr-tai-ray ser-see mwah-maim

Is there a left-luggage office?
Y a-t-il une consigne?
ee-ah-teel ewn kon-seen

Is there any charge?
Faut-il payer?
foh-teel pay-yay

No, do not put that on top
Non, ne mettez pas ça en haut
non, ner mai-tay pah sah ohn-oh

Please take these bags to a taxi
Portez ces valises à un taxi, s'il vous plaît
pohr-tay say vah-leez ah ern tahk-see, seel voo play

AT THE HOTEL

French hotels

In comparison with those in Britain, French hotels are good value – especially at the lower end of the market. But there are marked regional variations – the south coast is far more expensive than rural inland areas or other coasts of France.

The best-value hotels in France tend to be *auberges* or country inns. These are often delightful family-run establishments where they take pride in the quality of their food. In large towns and cities, the choice of hotels with character is not as good (Paris excepted) but you can nearly always find satisfactory chain hotels. At the luxury end of the market there are some splendid *châteaux*, beautifully converted mills, farms or priories – all elegantly furnished and often providing food of high quality.

Star ratings

Hotels in France are officially rated on a five-point scale, from simple one-star accommodation to four-star *de luxe*. (There are also basic unclassified hotels which are not categorised as *hôtels de tourisme*.) The French Tourist Office in London will provide you with a list of approved hotels. The star ratings are based on facilities (whether there's a lift, air conditioning, night porter, etc). They tell you roughly what prices to expect but give you no indication of what a place is really like.

Prices

Prices are controlled and should be displayed at reception and in every bedroom. Rates are quoted for the room, not per person, and are usually the same whether one or two people are using the room. Breakfast is rarely included in the price of the room. Rates include service and tax, except in some deluxe hotels where the service is charged separately. It is quite normal in any hotel to ask to see a room before you agree to take it.

Most hotels offer rates for *pension complète* (all three meals) and *demi-pension* (breakfast and one meal). To qualify for *pension complète* you usually have to stay for a minimum of three days and the meals may be different from the other restaurant menus – with less choice.

Meals

The normal French breakfast consists of French bread or croissants and coffee – '*café complet*'. You can usually have it in your room, and occasionally you have no choice but to do so.

Rooms and beds

Although the hotel will expect you to take its breakfast, there is no legal obligation to do so and you will find that the coffee and croissants are a lot cheaper in the local café – and often better too.

In the same way, many hotels will expect you to have an evening meal if you are staying the night, but under French law hoteliers are not allowed to insist that you do so. On the other hand, if it is a hotel that is renowned for its quality of cuisine you may not need to venture any farther.

Rooms and beds

In small hotels, double beds are the norm, though twins are becoming more common. In cheaper hotels, hard bolsters are used instead of pillows (but always check to see if there are pillows in the wardrobe) and there may be no soap provided.

A number of restaurants offer rooms that vary from basic to very luxurious. These restaurants-with-rooms are often very good value, but you cannot expect to stay in one unless you are planning to eat there.

Booking

Bookings for hotels need to be made well in advance during high season, particularly for Paris and other popular areas. In large towns, at stations and airports, there are offices known as *Accueil de France* which can book accommodation for you in their area or in main towns. Bookings can be made only up to a week ahead and for personal callers only.

Most hoteliers won't hold rooms after 6pm unless you've telephoned to say you will be late or have paid a deposit.

Bed and breakfast

With so many good-value hotels serving excellent food, it's not surprising that bed and breakfast has traditionally not been a prominent part of the French holiday scene. But that is changing, largely because the *Gîtes de France* organisation has set up a large-scale scheme to market bed and breakfast places. They're called *chambres d'hôtes*, and the roadside signs identifying them are now a common sight. The scheme promotes country homes offering bed and breakfast and 'a very warm family welcome' – ranging from cottages to small châteaux.

Another bed and breakfast organisation is *Café-Couette* (literally translated as Coffee-Duvet) offering over 1,000 homes to stay in. You are treated as one of the family and you can stay for as long as you like.

Guest membership of the organisation entitles you to the reservation service and the guide to all the bed and breakfasts available, in which they are graded from 2 to 5 'coffee pots'.

Reservations and enquiries

My name is…
Je m'appelle…
jer mah-pail

I have a reservation
J'ai réservé
jay ray-sair-vay

I am sorry I am late
Je suis en retard. Excusez-moi
jer swee zan rer-tahr. aiks-kew-say mwah

I was delayed at the airport
J'ai été retenu à l'aéroport
jay ay-tay rer-ter-new ah lahee-roh-pohr

My flight was late
Mon vol avait du retard
mon vohl ah-vay dew rer-tahr

I shall be staying until July 4th
Je reste jusqu'au quatre juillet
jer raist jews-koh kahtr joo-yay

I want to stay for 5 nights
Je veux rester cinq nuits
jer ver rais-tay sank nwee

Reservations and enquries

There are five of us
Nous sommes cinq
noo sohm sank

Do you have —a single room?
  Avez-vous —une chambre pour une personne?
  ah-vay voo — zewn shanbr poor ewn pair-sohn

—a double room with a bath?
  —une chambre pour deux personnes avec bain?
  — zewn shanbr poor der pair-sohn ah-vaik bern

—a room with twin beds and a shower?
  —une chambre avec lits jumeaux et douche?
  — zewn shanbr ah-vaik lee jew-moh ay doosh

I need — a double room with a bed for a child
Je veux — une chambre pour deux personnes avec un
         lit d'enfant.
*jer ver — ewn shanbr poor der pair-sohn ah-vaik ern
         lee dan-fan*

— a room with a double bed
  — une chambre avec un grand lit.
  — ewn shanbr ah-vaik ern gran lee

— a room with twin beds and bath
  — une chambre avec lits jumeaux et bain.
  — ewn shanbr ah-vaik lee jew-moh aybern

Reservations and enquiries

I need — a single room
Je veux — une chambre pour une personne.
jer ver — ewn shanbr poor ewn pair-sohn

— a single room with a shower or bath
— une chambre pour une personne avec
douche ou bain.
*— ewn shanbr poor ewn pair-sohn ah-vaik
doosh oo bern*

Does the price include — room and breakfast?
Est-ce que le tarif comprend — la chambre et le petit
déjeuner?
*ais-ker ler tah-reef kohm-pran — lah shanbr ay ler per-tee
day-jer-nay*

— room and all meals?
— la chambre et tous les
repas?
*— lah shanbr ay too lay rer-
pah*

— room and dinner?
— la chambre et le dîner?
— la shanbr ay ler dee-nay

How much is it for a child?
Cela coûte combien pour un enfant?
ser-lah koot kohm-byern poor ewn an-fan

How much is it — per night?
Combien coûte — par nuit?
kohm-byern koot — pahr nwee

— per person?
— par personne?
— pahr pair-sohn

— full board?
— la pension complète?
— lah pan-syon kohm-plait

— half-board?
— la demi-pension?
— lah der-mee pan-syon

Which floor is my room on?
A quel étage est ma chambre?
ah kail ay-tahj ai mah shanbr

Can we have breakfast in our room?
Pouvons-nous prendre le petit déjeuner dans la chambre?
poo-von noo prandr ler per-tee day-jer-nay dan la shanbr

Is this a safe area?
Est-ce que la région est sûre?
ais-ker lah ray-jeeon ai sewr

Can we have adjoining rooms?
Pouvons-nous avoir des chambres attenantes?
poo-von noo zah-vwahr day shanbr za-ter-nant

Reservations and enquries

Are there other children staying at the hotel?
Y a-t-il d'autres enfants à l'hôtel?
ee-ah-teel dohtr zan-fan ah loh-tail

Are there supervised activities for the children?
Y a-t-il des activités surveillées pour les enfants?
ee-ah-teel day zahk-tee-vee-tay sewr-vay-yay poor lay zan-fan

Can my son sleep in our room?
Est-ce que mon fils peut dormir avec nous?
ais-ke mon fees per dohr-meer ah-vaik noo

Is the voltage 220 or 110?
Est-ce que le courant est à 220 ou 110 volts?
ais-ker ler koo-ran ai ah der san van oo san dee vohlt

Is there a trouser press I can use?
Puis-je faire repasser mon pantalon?
pwee-jer fair rer-pah-say mon pan-tah-lon

Is there — a television?
Y a-t-il — un poste de télévision?
ee-ah-teel — ern pohst der tay-lay-vee-syon

— a hairdryer?
— un sèche-cheveux?
— ern saish-sher-ver

— a minibar?
— un minibar?
— ern mee-nee-bahr

Is there — a room service menu?
Y a-t-il — un menu servi dans les chambres?
ee-ah-teel — ern mer-new sair-vee dan lay shanbr

— a telephone?
— un téléphone?
— ern tay-lay-fohn

— a casino?
— un casino?
— ern kah-see-noh

— a lift?
— un ascenseur?
— ern ah-san-serr

— a sauna?
— un sauna?
— ern soh-nah

— a swimming pool?
— une piscine?
— ewn pee-seen

Do you have — a cot for my baby?
Avez-vous — un lit d'enfant pour mon bébé?
ah-vay voo — zan lee dan-fan poor mon bay-bay

— a laundry service?
— un service de blanchisserie?
— zern sair-vees der blan-shee-ser-ree

Reservations and enquiries

Do you have — a car park?
Avez-vous — un parking?
ah-vay voo — zern pahr-keeng

> **— a safe for valuables?**
> — un coffre pour les objets de valeur?
> *— ern kohfr poor lay-zohb-jay der vah-lerr*

> **— a fax machine?**
> — un télécopieur?
> *— zern tay-lay-koh-pee-err*

Is there — a market in the town?
Y a-t-il — un marché en ville?
ee-ah-teel — ern mahr-shay an veel

> **— a Chinese restaurant?**
> — un restaurant chinois?
> *— ern rais-toh-ran sheen-wah*

> **— a Vietnamese restaurant?**
> — un restaurant vietnamien?
> *— ern rais-toh-ran vyait-nah-myern*

Do you have satellite TV?
Recevez-vous les programmes par satellite?
rer-ser-vay voo lay proh-grahm pahr sah-tay-leet

What time — does the hotel close?
A quelle heure — est-ce que l'hôtel ferme?
ah kail err — ais-ker loh-tail fairm

38

What time — does the restaurant close?
A quelle heure — ferme le restaurant?
ah kail err — fairm ler rais-toh-ran

— is breakfast?
— est le petit déjeuner?
— ai ler per-tee day-jer-nay

— is lunch?
— est le déjeuner?
— ai ler day-jer-nay

— is dinner?
— est le dîner?
— ai ler dee-nay

— does the bar open?
— ouvre le bar?
— oovr ler bahr

Service

Please fill the minibar
Remplissez le minibar, s'il vous plaît
ran-plee-say ler mee-nee-bahr, seel voo play

Please send this fax for me
Transmettez ce fax, s'il vous plaît
trans-mai-tay ser fahks, seel voo play

Service

Please turn the heating off
Fermez le chauffage, s'il vous plaît
fair-may ler shoh-fahj, seel voo play

Please, wake me at 7 o'clock in the morning
Réveillez-moi à sept heures, s'il vous plaît
ray-vay-yay mwah ah sait err, seel voo play

Can I have — an ashtray?
Je peux avoir — un cendrier?
jer per ah-vwahr — ern san-dree-ay

— another blanket?
— une autre couverture?
— ewn ohtr koo-vair-tewr

— another pillow?
— un autre oreiller?
— ern ohtr oh-ray-yay

— my key, please?
— ma clef, s'il vous plaît?
— lah klay, seel voo play

— some coat hangers?
— des cintres?
— day serntr

— some note paper?
— du papier?
— dew pah-pyay

Can I have — a newspaper?
Je peux avoir — un journal?
jer per ah-vwahr — an joor-nahl

Can I have my wallet from the safe?
Je peux avoir mon portefeuille du coffre?
jer per ah-vwahr mon pohrt-fery dew kohfr

Can I hire a portable telephone?
Puis-je louer un téléphone portatif?
pweej loo-ay ern tay-lay-fohn pohr-tah-teef

Can I make a telephone call from here?
Puis-je téléphoner d'ici?
pweej tay-lay-foh-nay dee-see

Can I send this by courier?
Puis-je envoyer ceci par coursier?
pweej an-vwah-yay ser-see pahr koor-syay

Can I use my credit card?
Puis-je utiliser ma carte de crédit?
pweej ew-tee-lee-say mah kahrt der kray-dee

Can you connect me with the international operator?
Pouvez vous me passer la standardiste internationale?
poo-vay voo mer pah-say lah stan-dahr-deest an-tair-nah-syo-nahl

Service

Can I have an outside line, please?
Pouvez-vous me passer une ligne extérieure, s'il vous plaît?
poo-vay voo pah-say ewn leen aiks-tair-yerr, seel voo play

Can you recommend a good local restaurant?
Pouvez-vous me recommander un bon restaurant?
poo-vay voo mer rer-koh-man-day ern bon rais-toh-ran

Please charge this to my room
Mettez cela sur ma note, s'il vous plaît
mai-tay ser-lah sewr mah noht, seel voo play

Can I dial direct from my room?
Puis-je obtenir une ligne extérieure directement?
pweej ohb-ter-neer ewn leen aiks-tair-yerr dee-raik-ter-man

Can I use my personal computer here?
Puis-je utiliser mon PC ici?
pweej ew-tee-lee-say mon pay-say ee-see

I need an early morning call
Réveillez-moi de bonne heure
ray-vay-yay mwah der bohn err

I need — some soap
J'ai besoin — de savon
jay ber-zwern— der sah-von

— some towels
— de serviettes
— der sair-vyait

I need — a razor
J'ai besoin — d'un rasoir
jay ber-zwern— dern rah-zwahr

I need some toilet paper
Il me faut du papier hygiénique
eel mer foh dew pah-pyay ee-jay-neek

I need to charge these batteries
Je veux recharger ces piles
jer ver rer-shahr-jay say peel

I want to press these clothes
Je veux faire repasser ces vêtements
jer ver fair rer-pah-say say vait-man

Has my colleague arrived yet?
Est-ce que mon collègue est arrivé?
ais-ker mon koh-laig ai tah-ree-vay

How do I use the telephone?
Comment fait-on pour téléphoner?
koh-man fai-ton poor tay-lay-foh-nay

I am expecting a fax
J'attends un fax
jah-tan ern fahks

Where can I send a fax?
Où peut-on envoyer un fax?
oo per-ton an-vwah-yay ern fahks

Problems

What is the charge?
Quel est le tarif?
kail ai ler tah-reef

Problems

Can I speak to the manager?
Puis-je parler au directeur?
pweej pahr-lay oh dee-raik-terr

Where is the manager?
Où est le directeur?
oo ai ler dee-raik-terr

I cannot close the window
La fenêtre ne ferme pas
lah fer-naitr ner fairm pah

I cannot open the window
La fenêtre ne s'ouvre pas
lah fer-naitr ner soovr pah

The air conditioning is not working
La climatisation ne marche pas
lah klee-mah-tee-zah-syon ner mahrsh pah

The bathroom is dirty
La salle de bains est sale
lah sahl der bern ai sahl

The heating is not working
Le chauffage ne marche pas
ler shoh-fahj ner mahrsh pah

The light is not working
La lumière ne marche pas
lah lew-myair ner mahrsh pah

The room is not serviced
On ne fait pas le ménage dans la chambre
on ner fai pah ler may-nahj dan lah shanbr

The room is too noisy
La chambre est trop bruyante
lah shanbr ai troh broo-yant

The room key does not work
La clef de la chambre ne marche pas
lah klay der lah shanbr ner mahrsh pah

There are no towels in the room
Il n'y a pas de serviettes dans la chambre
eel nyah pah der sair-vyait dan lah shanbr

There is no hot water
Il n'y a pas d'eau chaude
eel nyah pah doh shohd

There is no plug for the washbasin
Il n'y a pas de bonde dans le lavabo
eel nyah pah der bond dan ler lah-vah-boh

Checking out

My daughter is ill
Ma fille est malade
mah fee ai mah-lahd

My son is lost
Mon fils s'est perdu
mon fees sai pair-dew

Checking out

Could you order me a taxi?
Appelez-moi un taxi, s'il vous plaît
ah-play mwah ern tahk-see, seel voo play

Please leave the bags in the lobby
Laissez les bagages dans le hall, s'il vous plaît
lay-say lay bah-gahj dan ler ahl, seel voo play

I want to stay an extra night
Je veux rester une nuit supplémentaire
jer ver rais-tay ewn nwee sew-play-man-tair

Do I have to change rooms?
Dois-je changer de chambre?
dwah jer shan-jay der shanbr

Can I have the bill please?
Puis-je avoir la note, s'il vous plaît?
pweej ah-vwahr lah noht, seel voo play

We will be leaving early tomorrow
Nous partons tôt demain matin
noo pahr-ton toh der-mern mah-tern

Thank you, we enjoyed our stay
Merci, nous avons fait un bon séjour
mair-see, noo zah-von fai tern bon say-joor

OTHER ACCOMMODATION

Self-catering

Self-catering holidays are very big business in France. There are simple rural cottages, stylish seaside villas, modern high-rise apartments, old farmhouses and barns – even apartments in grand *châteaux*.

Gîtes

Thousands of British families are now opting for holidays in *gîtes*. These are modestly priced simple country houses or apartments, offering a real taste of rural France. There are 30,000 altogether, many of them renovated farmhouses or country cottages. Some properties are quite remote, others in small villages, but there are very few which are not in rural locations and only a handful are near the sea. Properties are all inspected and graded by the *Gîtes de France* organisation but even the top-graded accommodation can't match the comforts of a 3-star hotel. What most *gîtes* can offer is rural charm and character. Each property is privately owned and sometimes the *gîte* may be a self-contained apartment in the owner's house.

Villas and apartments

The most popular area for villa and apartment holidays is the south of France. Here you find every type of holiday home, from studios and stylish villas to spanking new apartment blocks and Provençal-style cottages. In Languedoc-Roussillon the coast has been developed on a large scale with huge purpose-built complexes. Other popular coasts for self-catering are those of Brittany and the Atlantic.

Booking

If you want a *gîte* or any self-catering property in high season you must book well in advance. Seaside accommodation is usually snapped up by December or January, and even remote rural properties are booked up several months in advance. Lots of tour operators organise packages combining self-catering accommodation and car ferry, and there are also a number of air packages to the south of France.

Renting a house

We have rented this villa
Nous avons loué cette villa
noo zah-von loo-ee sait vee-lah

Renting a house

Here is our booking form
Voici notre bon de réservation
vwah-see nohtr bon der ray-sair-vah-syon

Can I contact you on this number?
Puis-je vous joindre à ce numéro?
pwee-jer voo jwandr ah ser new-may-roh

Can you send a repairman?
Pouvez-vous faire réparer?
poo-vay voo fair ray-pah-ray

How does this work?
Comment est-ce que ça marche?
koh-man ais-ker sah mahrsh

What is the voltage here?
Quelle est la tension, s'il vous plaît?
kail ai lah tan-syon, seel voo play

I cannot open the shutters
Les volets ne s'ouvrent pas
lay voh-lay ner soovr pah

Is the water heater working?
Est-ce que le chauffe-eau marche?
ais-ker ler shoh-foh mahrsh

Is the water safe to drink?
Est-ce que l'eau est potable?
ais-ker loh ai poh-tahbl

Renting a house

Is there any spare bedding?
Y a-t-il de la literie de rechange?
ee-ah-teel der lah lee-ter-ree der rer-shanj

The cooker does not work
La cuisinière ne marche pas
lah kwee-see-nyair ner mahrsh pah

The fridge does not work
Le frigo ne marche pas
ler free-goh ner mahrsh pah

The toilet is blocked
Les WC sont bouchés
lay doobl-vay-say son boo-shay

There is a leak
Il y a une fuite
eel-yah ewn fweet

We do not have any water
Nous n'avons pas d'eau
noo nah-von pah doh

We need two sets of keys
Il nous faut deux jeux de clefs
eel noo foh der jer der klay

When does the cleaner come?
La femme (**woman**)/l'agent (**man**) de ménage vient quand?
lah fahm/lah-jong der may-nahj vyern kan?

Around the house

Where is — the fuse box?
  Où est — la boîte à fusibles?
   oo ai — lah bwaht ah few-zeebl

— the bathroom?
  — la salle de bains?
   — lah sahl der bern

— the socket for my razor?
  — la prise pour le rasoir?
   — lah preez poor ler rah-zwahr

— the key for this door?
  — la clef de cette porte?
   — lah klay der sait pohrt

Around the house

bath
baignoire
bain-wahr

bathroom
salle de bains
sahl der bern

bed
lit
lee

brush
brosse
brohs

can opener
ouvre-boîte
oovr-bwaht

chair
chaise
shaiz

cooker
cuisinière
kwee-zee-nyair

corkscrew
tire-bouchon
teer-boo-shon

cup
tasse
tahs

fork
fourchette
foor-shait

fridge/refrigerator
frigo/frigidaire
free-goh/free-jee-dair

glass
verre
vair

kitchen
cuisine
kwee-zeen

knife
couteau
koo-toh

mirror
miroir
mee-rwahr

pan
casserole
kahs-rohl

plate
assiette
ass-yait

sheet
drap
drah

sink
évier
ay-vyay

spoon
cuillère
koo-yair

stove
cuisinière
kwee-see-nyair

table
table
tahbl

Camping

tap	**vacuum cleaner**
robinet	aspirateur
roh-bee-nay	*ahs-pee-rah-terr*
toilet	**washbasin**
toilettes	lavabo
twah-lait	*lah-vah-boh*

Camping

Camping is extremely popular in France, and the main sites are very well organised. The weather, particularly in the south, is well suited to the outdoor life and the facilities available at some of the sites make camping as comfortable as staying in a simple *gîte*. Tents with double beds, fridges, electric lights, gas stoves and even indoor chemical toilets are available for rent through UK tour operators.

Family camping holidays are increasingly popular. The sites are good places for getting to know people, and some put on organised activities to keep children amused. Such sites will have a restaurant or take-away food service for families who don't want to have to cook every meal.

Camping packages

There are several tour operators who offer all-in camping packages, the price inclusive of Channel ferry tickets and camping accommodation in pre-erected tents. The sites are usually very well organised and equipped. There are special rates for children. The overall price for a family works out at roughly the same as that of a *gîte* holiday.

Site gradings

Camp sites are classified from one to four stars, depending on the amenities. All sites are required by law to display their star rating and prices at the entrance. The camping charges are worked out according to the star ratings. On 1- and 2-star sites there are normally separate charges per person, per car, per caravan and per pitch: on 3- or 4-star sites there are often fixed charges per pitch, regardless of how many of you there are and what equipment you have. Charges usually run from midday to midday, and if you stay on a site after noon you will normally be charged for an extra night.

On the simplest sites the only facilities you can expect are covered washing and toilet areas (often inadequate for the number of campers), while at the other end of the market the big 4-star sites might have a pool, tennis courts, shops, launderette, restaurant, bar, playground and more. In other words, you don't have to move far to enjoy yourself – but you may find you're paying hotel prices.

All graded sites have a minimum space allocated to each pitch, although the restrictions tend to be ignored in high season. It's therefore worth checking out the size of your plot before deciding to take it.

Where to go

The most popular areas for camping are Brittany, Normandy, the Atlantic coast, the Dordogne and the south coast. The south has over 300 officially recognised sites, most of them offering attractive locations and good facilities. The sites on the Mediterranean are notoriously crowded in July and August and it's important to reserve your pitch in advance; if you don't enjoy being cheek-by-jowl with your neighbours, the Mediterranean sites are best avoided at this time.

For those who want 'to get away from it all', France has ample inland camping sites, providing privacy and peace. There are sites in the grounds of *châteaux*, in the fields of farmhouses, beside rivers, lakes and streams. Some of the town camp sites are surprisingly cheap and attractively located, often beside a river. In popular tourist areas, farms offer *camping à la ferme*, which is likely to be on a simple, quiet and uncrowded site.

Off-site camping, or *le camping sauvage*, is prohibited in many areas and notably in the south. There are areas of inland France where you can set up a tent – but always ask permission first.

Choosing a site

The best source for finding a site is the Michelin guide *Camping Caravaning France*. It is written in French, but the facilities are given in symbols and there are English translations where necessary. It recommends a wide range of sites and gives all the facilities available. The national camping organisation, the *Fédération Française de Camping Caravaning*, publishes another useful guide to camp sites.

For upmarket camping it's worth considering the *Castels et Caravaning* group, which offers accommodation at 40 4-star sites, many set in the grounds of *châteaux* and historic houses.

If you are travelling independently and wish to make a reservation, you can write direct to the camp sites, enclosing an International Reply Coupon (available from post offices). But remember that some of the smaller sites don't take advance bookings.

Before going it's worth buying an International Camping Carnet which shows you have third party insurance cover. Some upmarket sites won't let you in without it. The carnet is available from motoring, camping and caravanning organisations.

Useful camping phrases

Can we camp in your field?
Pouvons-nous camper dans votre champ?
poo-von noo kan-pay dan vohtr shan

Can we camp near here?
Pouvons-nous camper près d'ici?
poo-von noo kan-pay prai dee-see

Useful camping phrases

Can we park our caravan here?
Pouvons-nous garer notre caravane ici?
poo-von noo gah-ray nohtr kah-rah-vahn ee-see

Please can we pitch our tent here?
Pouvons-nous dresser notre tente ici?
poo-von noo drais-say nohtr tant ee-see

Where do I pay?
Où dois-je payer?
oo dwah jer pay-yay

Do I pay when I leave?
Dois-je payer au départ?
dwah-jer pay-yay oh day-pahr

Is there a more sheltered site?
Y a-t-il un emplacement plus abrité?
ee-ah-teel ern an-plahs-man plew zah-bree-tay

Is there a restaurant or a shop on the site?
Y a-t-il un restaurant ou un magasin sur place?
ee-ah-teel ern rais-toh-ran oo ern mah-gah-zan sewr plahs

Is there another campsite near here?
Y a-t-il un autre terrain de camping près d'ici?
ee-ah-teel ern ohtr tair-ran der kan-peeng prai dee-see

Is this the drinking water?
Est-ce bien l'eau potable?
ais byern loh poh-tahbl

Useful camping phrases

The site is very wet and muddy
L'emplacement est très humide et boueux
lan-plahs-man ai trai zew-meed ay boo-er

Where are the toilets?
Où sont les toilettes?
oo son lay twah-lait

Where can I have a shower?
Où puis-je prendre une douche?
oo pweej prandr ewn doosh

Where can we wash our dishes?
Où pouvons-nous faire notre vaisselle?
oo poo-von noo fair nohtr vai-sail

Is there — a paddling pool?
 Y a-t-il — une pataugeoire?
ee-ah-teel — ewn pah-toh-jwahr

— a swing park?
— des balançoires?
— day bah-lan-swahr

— a swimming pool?
— une piscine?
— ewn pee-seen

Around the camp site

air mattress
matelas pneumatique
maht-lah pner-mah-teek

backpack
sac à dos
sahk-ah-doh

bottle-opener
ouvre-bouteille
oovr-boo-tery

bucket
seau
soh

camp bed
lit de camp
lee der kan

camp chair
chaise pliante
shaiz plee-ant

candle
bougie
boo-jee

can-opener
ouvre-boîte
oovr-bwaht

cup
tasse
tahs

fire
feu
fer

flashlight
lampe électrique
lanp ay-laik-treek

fly sheet
double toit
doobl twah

folding table
table pliante
tahbl plee-ant

fork
fourchette
foor-shait

frying pan
poêle à frire
poh-ail ah freer

ground
sol
sohl

ground sheet
tapis de sol
tah-pee der sohl

guy line
corde
kohrd

knife
couteau
koo-toh

mallet
maillet
mah-yay

matches
allumettes
ah-lew-mait

pail
seau
soh

penknife
canif
kah-neef

plate
assiette
ah-syait

rucksack
sac à dos
sahk ah doh

shelter
abri
ah-bree

sleeping bag
sac de couchage
sahk der koo-shahj

spoon
cuillère
koo-yair

stove
cuisinière
kwee-zee-nyair

tent
tente
tant

Hostelling

tent peg
piquet de tente
pee-kay der tant

tent pole
montant de tente
mon-tan der tant

thermos flask
bouteille thermos
boo-tery tair-moh

torch
lampe électrique
lanp ay-laik-treek

Hostelling

Although often sited at the edge of town, or in difficult to reach rural areas, French youth hostels (*auberges de jeunesse*) provide good-value, basic accommodation for travellers on a budget, often in beautiful surroundings. As well as dormitory beds, rooms for couples are available in more modern hostels. To stay in a youth hostel you must be a member of the International Youth Hostel Federation (IYHF) or Hostelling International (HI). HI membership also covers two rival French youth hostel associations, the *Fédération Unie des Auberges de Jeunesse* and the *Ligue Française pour les Auberge de Jeunesse*.

Are you open during the day?
Etes-vous ouvert pendant la journée?
ait voo zoo-vair pan-dan lah joor-nay

What time do you close?
A quelle heure fermez-vous?
ah kail err fair-may voo

Can we stay five nights here?
Pouvons-nous rester ici cinq nuits?
poo-von noo rais-tay ee-see sank nwee

Can we stay until Sunday?
Pouvons-nous rester jusqu'à dimanche?
poo-von noo rais-tay jews-kah dee-mansh

Do you serve meals?
Servez-vous des repas?
sair-vay voo day rer-pah

Can I use the kitchen?
Puis-me me servir de la cuisine?
pweej mer sair-veer der lah kwee-zeen

Here is my membership card
Voici ma carte de membre
vwah-see mah kahrt der manbr

I do not have my card
Je n'ai pas ma carte sur moi
jer nay pah mah kahrt sewr mwah

Can I join here?
Puis-je m'inscrire ici?
pweej mern-skreer ee-see

Thank you, we enjoyed our stay
Merci, nous avons fait un bon séjour
mair-see, noo zah-von fai tern bon say-joor

Childcare

Can you warm this milk for me?
Pouvez-vous faire réchauffer ce lait, s'il vous plaît?
poo-vay voo fair ray-shoh-fay ser lai, seel voo play

Do you have a cot for my baby?
Avez-vous un lit d'enfant pour mon bébé?
ah-vay voo zan lee dan-fan poor mon bay-bay

Do you have a high chair?
Avez-vous une chaise haute?
ah-vay voo zewn shaiz oht

Is there a baby-sitter?
Y a-t-il une baby-sitter?
ee-ah-teel ewn bay-bay-see-tair?

My daughter is 7 years old
Ma fille a sept ans
mah fee ah sait an

My son is 10 years old
Mon fils a dix ans
mon fees ah dee zan

She goes to bed at nine o'clock
Elle se couche à neuf heures
ail ser koosh ah ner verr

Childcare

We will be back in two hours
Nous serons de retour dans deux heures
noo ser-ron der rer-toor dan der zerr

Where can I buy some disposable nappies?
Où puis-je trouver des couches à jeter?
oo pweej troo-vay day koosh ah jer-tay

Where can I change the baby?
Où puis-je changer le bébé?
oo pweej shan-jay ler bay-bay

Where can I feed my baby?
Où puis-je nourrir mon bébé?
oo pweej noo-reer mon bay-bay

I am very sorry. That was very naughty of him
Je suis désolé : il a été très vilain
jer swee day-soh-lay : eel ah ay-tay trai vee-lern

It will not happen again
Cela ne se reproduira pas
ser-lah ner ser rer-proh-dwee-rah

GETTING AROUND

Public transport

France has a very comprehensive rail system covering the whole country. The SNCF (*Société Nationale de Chemins de Fer*), a nationally owned company, runs a fast, efficient, modern service. The TGV (*Train à Grande Vitesse*) is the fastest train in the world – from Paris to Lyon it takes just 2 hours, which means that from city centre to city centre it is faster than going by air. Bus services are mainly used to connect rural areas to the rail network. The inland air service is useful for very long journeys, particularly those not covered by high-speed trains. Public transport can be prone to disruption by strikes.

Getting around Paris

If you arrive by air at Charles de Gaulle airport, the easiest way to get to the centre of Paris is to take the airport coach to Porte Maillot, near the Place de l'Etoile. The cheaper alternative is to take the shuttle bus to Charles de Gaulle station, then a train to the Gare du Nord. If you arrive by train you can get straight on to the Métro system.

The Métro and the RER (*Réseau Express Régional*) suburban lines are quick, efficient and cheap. The system is quite simple as long as you remember that the lines are called by the names of the station at each end (there are two names for each line). When you want to change trains you follow signs saying *Correspondances*. Electronic maps will help you pinpoint the station you want and the fastest route to take. If you are making several journeys, a book of 10 tickets (called a *carnet*) works out cheaper than buying them individually. One ticket takes you as far as you want. There are also *Paris Visites* visitor's passes that allow unlimited travel for 2, 3 or 5 days around Paris and its suburbs. A *Carte Orange* (you'll need a passport photo) is valid from Monday to Sunday and allows unlimited travel within specific zones.

Buses are a less convenient form of transport than the Métro but may be preferable for the tourist because you get to see the layout of the city.

Asking for directions

Excuse me, please
Excusez-moi, s'il vous plaît
aik-skew-say mwah, seel voo play

Where is — the art gallery?
Où est — la galerie d'art?
oo ai — lah gah-lai-ree dahr

Asking for directions

Where is — the police station?
Où est — le commissariat de police?
oo ai — ler koh-mee-sah-ryah der poh-lees

— the post office?
— le bureau de poste?
— ler bew-roh der pohst

Can you tell me the way to the bus station?
Où est la gare routière?
oo ai lah gahr roo-tyair

Can you show me on the map?
Montrez-moi sur le plan, s'il vous plaît
mon-tray mwah sewr ler plan, seel voo play

I am looking for the Tourist Information Office
Je cherche l'Office de Tourisme
jer shairsh loh-fees der too-reesm

I am lost
Je suis perdu
jer swee pair-dew

I am lost. How do I get to the Hôtel de la Gare?
Je suis perdu. Où se trouve l'hôtel de la Gare?
jer swee pairdew. oo ser troov loh-tail der lah gahr

I am trying to get to the market
Je cherche le marché
jer shairsh ler mahr-shay

I want to go to the theatre
Je veux aller au théâtre
jer ver ah-lay oh tay-ahtr

Is this the right way to the supermarket?
C'est bien par ici, le supermarché?
sai byern pahr ee-see, ler sew-pair-mahr-shay

We are looking for a restaurant
Nous cherchons un restaurant
noo shair-shon zern rais-toh-ran

Where are the toilets?
Où sont les toilettes?
oo son lay twah-lait

Where do I get a bus for the city centre?
D'où part le bus pour le centre-ville?
doo pahr ler bews poor ler santr veel

How long does it take to get to the park?
Il y en a pour combien de temps pour aller au parc?
eel yan ah poor kohm-byern der tan poor ah-lay oh pahrk

Is it far?
Est-ce loin?
ais lwern

Can you walk there?
On peut y aller à pied?
on per tee ah-lay ah pyay?

By road

Where does this road go to?
Où mène cette route?
oo main sait root

Which road do I take to Bordeaux?
Quelle est la route de Bordeaux?
kail ai lah root der bohr-doh

How do I get onto the motorway (highway)?
Comment peut-on rejoindre l'autoroute (la grande route)?
koh-man per-ton rer-jwandr loh-toh-root (lah grand root)

How far is it to Nancy?
Il y a combien de kilomètres jusqu'à Nancy?
eel yah kohm-byern der kee-loh-maitr jewsk-ah nan-see

How long will it take to get there?
Dans combien de temps y serai-je?
dan kohm-byern der tan ee ser-raij

I am looking for the next exit
Je cherche la prochaine sortie
jer shairsh lah proh-shain sohr-tee

Is there a filling station near here?
Y a-t-il un poste d'essence près d'ici?
ee-ah-teel ern pohst dai-sans prai dee-see

Which is the best route to Lyon?
Quelle est la meilleure route pour aller à Lyon?
kail ai lah mai-yerr root poor ah-lay ah lee-on

Which is the fastest route?
Quelle est la route la plus rapide?
kail ai lah root lah plew rah-peed

Directions

Vous allez — à gauche
voo zah-lay— ah gohsh
    You go — left

        — à droite
        — ah drwaht
        — right

        — jusqu'à
        — jewsk-kah
        — as far as…

        — vers...
        — vair...
        — towards…

        — juste à côté
        — jewst ah koh-tay
        — around the corner

Directions

Continuez tout droit
kon-tee-nway too drwah
Keep going straight ahead

Suivez la direction — de l'autoroute
swee-vay lah dee-raik-syon — der loh-toh-root
Follow the signs for — the motorway

— du prochain carrefour
— dew proh-shern kahr-foor
— the next junction

Tournez à gauche
toor-nay ah gohsh
Turn left

Tournez à droite
toor-nay ah drwaht
Turn right

C'est — au carrefour
sai — toh kahr-foor
It is — at the intersection

— à côté du cinéma
— ah koh-tay dew see-nay-mah
— next to the cinema

— à l'étage au-dessus/à l'étage au-dessous
— ah lay-tahj oh der-sew/ ah lay-tahj oh der-soo
— on the next floor (up)/on the next floor (down)

72

C'est — en face de la gare
  sai — an fahs der lah gahr
  It is — opposite the railway station

      — là-bas
      — lah-bah
      — over there

Il faut régler le péage
eel foh ray-glay ler pay-ahj
You have to pay the toll

Prenez la première à droite
prer-nay lah prer-myair ah drwaht
Take the first road on the right

Prenez la route d'Albi
prer-nay lah root dahl-bee
Take the road for Albi

Prenez la deuxième à gauche
prer-nay lah der-zyaim ah gohsh
Take the second road on the left

Hiring a car

It is cheaper to organise the rental of a car before you leave home, but you can rent cars at airports and in most cities (there may be a surcharge included at the airport). Basic car insurance

Hiring a car

will be included in the rental fee, but beware of being sold
unneccesary cover that may already be included in your travel
insurance.

I want to hire a car
Je veux louer une voiture
jer ver loo-ay ewn vwah-tewr

Can I hire a car?
Puis-je louer une voiture?
pweej loo-ay ewn vwah-tewr

Can I hire a car with an automatic gearbox?
Puis-je louer une automatique?
pweej loo-ay ewn oh-toh-mah-teek

Can I pay for insurance?
Puis-je payer l'assurance?
pweej pay-yay lah-sew-rans

Do I have to pay a deposit?
Dois-je verser des arrhes?
dwah-jer vair-say day zahr

Do I pay in advance?
Dois-je payer d'avance?
dwah-jer pay-yay dah-vans

Is tax included?
Est-ce que la taxe est comprise?
ais-ker lah tahks ai kohm-preez

Is there a charge per kilometre?
Y a-t-il un tarif par kilomètre?
ee-ah-teel ern tah-reef pahr kee-loh-maitr

Do you have — a large car?
  Avez-vous — une grosse voiture?
  ah-vay voo — zewn grohs vwah-tewr

> **— a smaller car?**
> — une voiture plus petite?
> *— zewn vwah-tewr plew per-teet*

> **— an automatic?**
> — une automatique?
> *— zewn oh-toh-mah-teek*

> **— an estate car?**
> — un break?
> *— zan braik*

I need it for 2 weeks
J'en ai besoin pour deux semaines
john ay ber-zwan poor der ser-main

We will both be driving
Nous conduirons tous les deux
noo kohn-dwe-ron too lay der

I need to complete this form
Je dois remplir ce formulaire
jer dwah ran-pleer ser fohr-mew-lair

Hiring a car

I want to leave the car at the airport
Je veux laisser la voiture à l'aéroport
jer ver lai-say lah vwah-tewr ah lai-roh-pohr

I would like a spare set of keys
Je voudrais un jeu de clefs de rechange
jer voo-drai ern jer der klay der rer-shanj

Must I return the car here?
Faut-il ramener la voiture ici?
foh-teel rahm-nay lah vwah-tewr ee-see

Please explain the documents
Expliquez-moi ces documents, s'il vous plaît
aiks-plee-kay mwah say doh-kew-man, seel voo play

Please show me how to operate the lights
Montrez-moi comment fonctionnent les phares
mon-tray mwah koh-man fon-syonn lay fahr

Please show me how to operate the windscreen wipers
Montrez-moi comment fonctionnent les essuie-glace
mon-tray mwah koh-man fon-syonn lay zai-swee-glahs

Where is reverse gear?
Où est la marche arrière?
oo ai lah mahrsh ah-ryair

Where is the tool kit?
Où est la trousse à outils?
oo ai lah troos ah oo-tee?

How does the steering lock work?
Comment fonctionne l'antivol de direction?
koh-man fon-syohn lan-tee-vohl der dee-raik-syon

By taxi

As in this country, taxis can be picked up at a rank or will stop if you hail them. A tip of a few francs is expected.

Where can I get a taxi?
Où puis-je trouver un taxi?
oo pwee-jer troo-vay ern tahk-see?

Please show us around the town
Faites-nous faire un tour de la ville, je vous prie
fait noo fair ern toor der lah veel, jer voo pree

Please take me to this address
Conduisez-moi à cette adresse, s'il vous plaît
kon-dwee-zay mwah ah sait ah-drais, seel voo play

How much is it per kilometre?
C'est combien le kilomètre?
sai kohm-byern ler kee-loh-maitr?

Will you put the bags in the boot?
Mettez les valises dans le coffre, s'il vous plaît
mai-tay lay vah-leez dan ler kohfr, seel voo play

By taxi

Please wait here for a few minutes
Attendez ici quelques minutes, s'il vous plaît
ah-tan-day ee-see kail-ker mee-newt, seel voo play

Please, stop at the corner
Arrêtez-vous au coin, s'il vous plaît
ah-rai-tay voo oh kwern, seel voo play

Please, wait here
Veuillez patienter un moment
ver-yay pah-syan-tay an moh-man

Take me to the airport, please
Conduisez-moi à l'aéroport, s'il vous plaît
kon-dwee-zay mwah ah lai-roh-pohr, seel voo play

The bus station, please
La gare routière, s'il vous plaît
lah gahr roo-tyair, seel voo play

I am in a hurry
Je suis pressé
jer swee prai-say

Please hurry, I am late
Depêchez-vous, je suis en retard
day-pai-shay voo, jer swee zan rer-tahr

Turn left, please
Tournez à gauche, s'il vous plaît
toor-nay ah gohsh, seel voo play

Turn right, please
Tournez à droite, s'il vous plaît
toor-nay ah drwaht, seel voo play

Wait for me please
Attendez-moi, s'il vous plaît
ah-tan-day mwah, seel voo play

Can you come back in one hour?
Pouvez-vous revenir dans une heure?
poo-vay voo rer-ver-neer dan zewn err

How much is that, please?
C'est combien, s'il vous plaît?
sai kohm-byern, seel voo play

Keep the change
Gardez la monnaie
gahr-day lah moh-nay

By bus

The most reliable bus services in France follow the SNCF network, and are useful for local journeys and connections to stations. In most cities they will operate a pay-as-you-enter system and accept travel cards. Privately run services to rural areas that are not reachable by a railway are sometimes infrequent and unreliable.

By bus

Does this bus go to the castle?
Est-ce que ce bus va au château?
ais-ker ser bews vah oh shah-toh

How frequent is the service?
Quelle est la fréquence du service?
kail ai lah fray-kans dew sair-vees

What is the fare to the city centre?
C'est combien pour le centre-ville?
sai kohm-byern poor ler santr veel

When is the last bus?
Quand part le dernier bus?
kan pahr ler dair-nyay bews

Where do I get the bus for the airport?
D'où part le bus pour l'aéroport?
doo pahr ler bews poor lai-roh-pohr

Which bus do I take for the football stadium?
Quel bus faut-il prendre pour aller au stade?
kail bews foh-teel prandr poor ah-lay oh stahd

Please tell me when to get off the bus
Dites-moi où je dois descendre, s'il vous plaît
deet mwah oo jer dwah day-sandr

By train

Travelling by Eurostar through the Channel Tunnel will take you directly from London Waterloo to Lille in about two hours, and to Paris Gard du Nord in about three hours.

The rail system in France is generally reliable and efficient. The TGV now extends over a wide network, including Lille, Rouen and Nice. The ride in the TGVs (and in the slower long-distance Corail trains) is smooth and comfortable. Prices are reasonable and trains normally arrive on time.

Reservations can be made in Britain – check with your travel agent. In France they can be made at main railway stations or by telephone. Advance bookings for the TGV are compulsory but you can make these up to a few minutes before departure at special machines at the station.

All tickets bought in France must be validated at the orange machines at the entrance to the platform before you travel and again if you make a break in your journey of more than 24 hours.

For off-peak travel there are discounts. If you intend to make several train journeys, it's worth purchasing a *Euro Domino* ticket, giving unlimited travel on any 3, 5 or 10 days in a month and entitling you to a reduction on Eurostar. Rail cards that give a reduction can also be bought: for couples (*Carte Couple*, 25 per cent reduction), people over 60 (*Carte Vermeille*, 30 per cent reduction), people under 26 (*Carissimo*, 30 per cent reduction) and children under 16 (*Carte Kiwi*, 30 per cent reduction for ticket holder and up to four others of any age).

By train

When is the next train to Calais?
Quand part le prochain train pour Calais?
kan pahr ler proh-shern trern poor kah-lay

Where can I buy a ticket?
Où puis-je acheter un billet?
oo pweej ash-tay ern bee-yay

Can I buy a return ticket?
Puis-je prendre un aller-retour?
pweej prandr ern ah-lay-rer-toor

A return (round-trip ticket) to Toulouse, please
Un aller-retour pour Toulouse, s'il vous plaît
ern ah-lay-rer-toor poor too-looz, seel voo play

A return to Paris, first class
Un aller-retour pour Paris, en première classe
ern ah-lay-rer-toor poor pah-ree, an prer-myair klahs

A single (one-way ticket) to Montpellier, please
Un aller simple pour Montpellier, s'il vous plaît
ern ah-lay-sernpl poor mon-per-lyay, seel voo play

A smoking compartment, first-class
Compartiment fumeurs, première classe
kohm-pahr-tee-man few-merr, prer-myair klahs

A non-smoking compartment, please
Compartiment non-fumeurs, s'il vous plaît
kohm-pahr-tee-man non-few-merr, seel voo play

Second class. A window seat, please
Deuxième classe. Côté fenêtre, s'il vous plaît
der-zyaim klahs. koh-tay fer-naitr, seel voo play

I have to leave tomorrow
Je dois partir demain
jer dwah pahr-teer der-man

I want to book a seat on the sleeper to Paris
Je veux réserver une couchette dans le train de Paris
jer ver ray-sair-vay ewn koo-shait dan ler trern der pah-ree

What are the times of the trains to Paris?
Quels sont les horaires des trains pour Paris?
kail son lay zoh-rair day trern poor pah-ree

Where is the departure board (listing)?
Où est le tableau des départs?
oo ai ler tah-bloh day day-pahr

Where should I change?
Où faut-il changer?
oo foh-teel shan-jay

Can I take my bicycle?
Puis-je emmener mon vélo?
pweej an-mer-nay mon vay-loh

Is there — a restaurant on the train?
Y a-t-il — un restaurant dans le train?
ee-ah-teel — ern rais-toh-ran dan ler trern

By train

Is there — a buffet car (club car)?
Y a-t-il — un buffet?
ee-ah-teel — ern bew-fay

— a dining car?
— un wagon-restaurant?
— ern vah-gon rais-toh-ran

Do I have time to go shopping?
Ai-je le temps de faire des courses?
ay-jer ler tan der fair day koors

Which platform do I go to?
C'est sur quel quai?
sai sewr kail kay

How long do I have before my next train leaves?
Il me reste combien de temps avant le prochain train?
eel mer raist kohm-byern der tan ah-van ler proh-shern trern

What time does the train leave?
A quelle heure part le train?
ah kail err pahr ler trern

What time is the last train?
A quelle heure part le dernier train?
ah kail err pahr ler dair-nyay trern

Where do I have to change?
Où faut-il changer?
oo foh-teel shan-jay

Is this the Marseilles train?
C'est bien le train de Marseille?
sai byern ler trern der mahr-say

Is this the platform for Grenoble?
C'est bien le quai pour le train de Grenoble?
sai byern ler kay poor ler trern der grer-nohbl

Is this a through train?
Est-ce un train direct?
ais ern trern dee-raikt

Are we at Orléans yet?
Sommes-nous arrivés à Orléans?
sohm noo zah-ree-vay ah ohr-lay-an

What time do we get to Nantes?
A quelle heure arrivons-nous à Nantes?
ah kail err ah-ree-von noo zah nant

Do we stop at Le Mans?
Est-ce que le train s'arrête au Mans?
ais-ker ler trern sah-rait oh man

Are we on time?
On est à l'heure?
on ais tah lerr

How long will the delay be?
Combien de temps faudra-t-il attendre?
kohm-byern der tan foh-drah-teel ah-tandr

By train

How long will this take?
Il y en a pour combien de temps?
eel yan ah poor kohm-byern der tan

Can you help me with my bags?
Pouvez-vous m'aider avec mes bagages?
poo-vay voo may-day ah-vaik may bah-gahj

I want to leave these bags in the left-luggage
Je veux laisser ces bagages à la consigne
jer ver lai-say say bah-gahj ah lah kon-seen

I shall pick them up this evening
Je reviendrai les prendre ce soir
jer rer-vyern-drai lay prandr ser swahr

How much is it per bag/case?
C'est combien par sac/valise?
sai kohm-byern parh sahk/va-leez

May I open the window?
Puis-je ouvrir la fenêtre?
pweej oov-reer lah fer-naitr

Is this seat taken?
Est-ce que cette place est libre?
ais ker sait plahs ai leebr

My wife has my ticket
C'est ma femme qui a mon billet
sai mah fahm kee ah mon bee-yay

I have lost my ticket
J'ai perdu mon billet
jay pair-dew mon bee-yay

This is a non-smoking compartment
C'est un compartiment non-fumeurs
sai tern kohm-pahr-tee-man non-few-merr

This is my seat
C'est ma place
sai mah plahs

Where is the toilet?
Où sont les toilettes?
oo son lay twah-lait

Why have we stopped?
Pourquoi avons-nous stoppé?
poor-kwah ah-von noo stoh-pay

DRIVING

Driving

Driving in France is quite straightforward and can even be pleasurable. Most of the roads (even minor ones) are fast, straight and uncrowded – for most of the time, anyway – and traffic congestion is much less severe than in Britain. Getting used to driving on the right is not as big a problem as it may at first seem.

France has an impressively comprehensive network of motorways, though most have only two lanes per carriageway. Tolls are charged on almost all of them, and these can mount up to considerable sums. On high-summer weekends it's important to steer clear of the notorious traffic blackspots: the Paris ring-road and the motorway from Paris via Beaune and Lyon to the south.

The roads

There are two main types of ordinary road: a *route nationale* (national road), prefixed with an N, and a *route départementale* ('county' road), prefixed with a D. Many of the N roads have become D roads in the last few years, and although you'll find the new numbers indicated on up-to-date maps, a lot of the signposts haven't yet been changed and some maps are still out of date. The more important N roads – the country's major arteries before the motorways were built – are often straight and fast but can be very hazardous, particularly where they go through towns and villages.

Motorways paying tolls

Normally as you approach a motorway you'll be confronted by a number of gates: head for one with a green light, press a button and take the ticket that emerges. It records where you joined the motorway and determines how much you pay when you leave it. There are occasional toll barriers across the main motorways – usually as you approach a city – where there may be short stretches that are free or for which you pay a fixed charge. If you have the correct change you can opt to go through an automatic gate where you toss coins into a chute as you drive through. At manned booths you can pay by Eurocheque, and on some motorways Visa credit cards are accepted.

Service areas

Motorway service areas often have impressive catering facilities – a single service area may have everything from a snack-bar serving fresh-ground coffee and croissants to a waiter-service restaurant with four-course menus. The best-value meals are the *routier* ('truck-driver') menus. Holders

Route-finding

of the current *Relais Routier Guide* can get a four-course meal with beer, mineral water or a quarter litre of wine for under ten pounds. Service areas are quite frequent, but in between you will often find an *aire de repos* – a rest area with parking, toilets (not always too salubrious) and probably a picnic area with a rustic bench or two.

Route-finding

French motorways are notorious for horrendous traffic jams at peak holiday times. But most holiday destinations can be reached using less crowded alternative routes, or *Itineraires Bis,* indicated by green arrows on white (north to south) and white on green (south to north). The alternative network is marketed under the name *Bison Futé* ('crafty bison'); there are free *Bison Futé* maps available at toll booths, information centres and some service areas. Watch for the *Bison Futé* signs – a Red Indian who is supposed to know when the palefaces (tourists) will be on the warpath. Watch out also for yellow arrows on blue, labelled *itineraires de délestage*, showing shorter alternative routes for avoiding traffic blackspots at peak periods.

Route-planning maps

The Michelin route-planning map, sheet 911, covers dozens of alternative routes through France using the extensive network of secondary roads (as well as motorways and major roads, of course). In addition there's information on distances and driving times between towns and the peak holiday times to avoid. Map 915, in booklet form, covers the major routes for the whole of France. An English version of the useful *Bison Futé* brochure is available from the French Tourist Office, ferry ports and the AA and RAC.

Touring maps

For use once you've arrived in a particular area, there are three good series of maps available. The yellow-covered Michelin maps, which have a scale of 2km to 1cm, have the advantage that they link with the Michelin Red Guide, identifying towns and villages that have an entry in the guide and so greatly simplifying the job of finding a good hotel or restaurant when you're on the road.

The two other series both have a scale of 2.5km to 1cm, covering a bit more ground in a given area of map. The excellent maps published in France by Recta Foldex are now widely available in Britain under the *Telegraph* name: they have an index of place-names printed on the back. The maps published by the *IGN* (the French equivalent of the Ordnance Survey) are also good but are sold here only in fairly specialist shops.

Town plans

Even if you don't plan to do much eating out, the *Michelin Red Guide* to hotels and restaurants is worth buying for its many invaluable town plans. The regional *Michelin Green Guides* (for sightseeing) also have some town plans. The plans in both types of guide are linked to the Michelin yellow-covered maps by a common system of numbering the main roads into each town.

The rules

The main rules

Driving on the right It's surprising how quickly you get used to the idea of hugging the right-hand kerb. The real danger comes when you stop, usually for petrol: if you drive out from the petrol station on to a deserted road, your instinct may be to begin driving on the left-hand side.

Priority to the right *Priorité à droite* (giving way to traffic on your right) is being phased out. Most main roads now have priority, indicated by a succession of yellow diamond signs with white borders; when you lose priority the yellow sign has a black bar across it.

Roundabouts

The *priorité* rule used to mean that cars approaching a roundabout had priority over those already on it. In 1984 the system was changed to give priority to cars already on the roundabout, with prominent signs on the approach roads saying *Vous n'avez pas la priorité* – 'you do not have priority'. Even so, you still have to watch out for tiny roundabouts –

perhaps going round a village monument – where the old rules still apply.

Speed limits

Speed limits are slightly higher than in Britain except when it's wet. They are now quite strictly enforced. Exceeding the speed limit can result in an on-the-spot cash fine as large as 5000 francs.

Open roads Unless road signs say otherwise, the following general limits apply: 90km/hr (56mph) on ordinary roads, 110km/hr (68mph) on dual carriageways and toll-free motorways and 130km/hr (80mph) on toll motorways. When it's wet, and for drivers with less than two years' experience, the limits are lowered to 110km/hr (68mph) on toll motorways and 80km/hr (50mph) on other roads. There is a minimum speed limit of 80km/hr (50mph) in the outside lane of motorways during daylight.

Towns The limit in built-up areas is 60km/hr (37mph); the place-name sign marks the beginning of a town for speed-limit purposes; the end is marked by the name crossed out with a red line.

Other rules

You have to be 18 to drive a car; and you can't drive on a British provisional licence.

Drinking and driving is vigorously policed. Random breath-testing is widespread, and fines can be high: pleading ignorance will get you nowhere. A conviction can affect your

The rules

insurance rating in Britain and can result in a prison sentence in France. It's worth remembering that spirit measures in French cafés are twice as large as those in British pubs.

Safety belts are compulsory for the driver and front-seat passenger: if safety belts are fitted to the rear seats, passengers in those seats must use them; under-tens must not travel in the front seat of a car that has a back seat.

Overtaking on the brow of a hill is not permitted. After overtaking on a multi-lane road you must return to the inside lane.

Stopping on open roads is not allowed unless you can drive right off the road.

Fines There's a system of on-the-spot fines for many motoring offences. To be accurate, it's not a fine but a deposit system, and the police collect the money only from people who can't show that they are resident in France. You have to pay in cash and the amounts are steep. Theoretically, you can always attend the subsequent court hearing: if you're not found guilty your deposit will be returned.

Parking The rules are similar to those in Britain, except that instead of yellow lines on the road, you should look for yellow marks on the kerbs. In some town streets parking is allowed on one side early in the month and on the other late in the month.

An area controlled by parking meters or automatic ticket machines is called a *zone grise* ('grey zone'): you have to pay to park between 9.00am and 7.00pm. In most large towns you can park in a *zone bleue* ('blue zone') between 9.00am and

12.30pm, and 2.30pm and 7.00pm. You have to display a time disc, which allows up to an hour's parking. You can buy discs from police stations; some shops and tourist offices will give you one free.

On the road

Breakdowns Move the car to the verge and either switch on the hazard warning lights or put the red warning triangle about 30m behind the car (100m on a motorway). On a motorway, call the police from an emergency telephone – there's one every 2km. On other roads, it will normally be best to find the nearest garage, though you can ring the police if necessary (telephone number 17). The local *garagiste* is often a friendly and highly competent mechanic who will charge you very modest prices. Main dealers of major brands of car are listed for each town in the Michelin Red Guide. The AA publish a useful *Car Components Guide,* translating the names of nearly 500 car parts with illustrations.

Accidents Inform the police, particularly if someone is injured (telephone 17). Motorists involved in an accident must complete a *constat à l'amiable* (accident statement form). If one or other party refuses to sign, then the case is taken to a local *huissier* (bailiff) who prepares a written report called a *constat d'huissier.* This may take several days and can be expensive.

Filling up If you ask for the tank to be filled, make sure you don't get charged for more than you've had. It's safer to specify

Road signs

how much you want, in francs if you prefer – e.g. *pour cin-quante francs.*

Self-service stations (which are not very common in France) are invariably cheaper than those with attendants, and petrol costs quite a lot more on motorways than on normal roads.

The most useful credit card is Visa (*Carte Bleue*), but acceptance is far from universal. Acceptance of Access cards is slowly improving.

Types of fuel *Pétrole* in French means crude oil or paraffin; *essence* graded *normale* or *super* is the stuff you put in the car – though the word *essence* alone will often be taken to mean *normale.* Octane ratings are not always shown on pumps: *normale is* 90 octane, a low 2-star; *super is* 98 octane, 4-star. Watch out for *super sans plomb,* unleaded petrol.

Road signs

Road sign symbols are more or less international these days, but there are a lot of written signs in France that you might not be familiar with. The main ones are given below. If you're going through a town and there are no signs pointing to the destination you want, follow signs saying *autres directions* (other directions) or *toutes directions* (all directions).

absence de marquage — no road markings

accotements non stabilisés/consolidés — soft verge

agglomération — built-up area

aire de service (de repos) — service (rest) area

autoroute à péage — toll motorway

attention aux travaux — danger – road works

autres directions — other directions

bifurcation — road fork

bouchon — bottleneck

boue — mud

cédez le passage — give way

centre-ville — town centre

chantier (travaux) — roadworks

chaussée déformée — poor road surface

chute de pierres — (possibility of) fallen stones

défense de stationner — no parking

déviation — diversion

éboulement — landslide

entrée interdite — no entry

essence — petrol

éteignez vos phares/feux — switch off lights

feux — traffic lights

fin de — end of

gravillons — loose chippings

interdit sauf aux livraisons (riverains) — no entry except for deliveries (residents)

itinéraire bis — alternative route

passage protégé — your right of way

péage — toll

poids lourds — heavy vehicles

priorité à droite — priority to the right

Traffic and weather conditions

préparez votre monnaie — get your change ready

prochaine sortie — next exit

ralentir — slow down

route barrée — road closed

sens unique — one-way street

serrez à droite — keep to the right

sortie — exit

stationnement — parking

toutes directions — all directions

travaux — roadworks

un train peut en cacher un autre — (at level crossings)
one train can hide another coming the other way

véhicules lents — slow vehicles

verglas — ice on road

virages — bends

voie sans issue — no through road

Traffic and weather conditions

Are there any hold-ups?
Y a-t-il des bouchons?
ee-ah-teel day boo-shon

Is the traffic one-way?
Est-ce une route à sens unique?
ais ewn root ah sans ew-neek

Traffic and weather conditions

Is the pass open?
Est-ce que le col est ouvert?
ais ker ler kohl ai too-vair

Is the road to Annecy snowed up?
Est-ce que la route d'Annecy est enneigée?
ais ker lah root dahn-see ai tan-nai-jay

Is the traffic heavy?
Y a-t-il beaucoup de circulation?
ee-ah-teel boh-koo der seer-kew-lah-syon

Is there a different way to the stadium?
Y a-t-il une autre route pour aller au stade?
ee-ah-teel ewn ohtr root poor ah-lay oh stahd

Is there a toll on this motorway (highway)?
Est-ce que cette autoroute (route) est à péage?
ais ker sait oh-toh-root (root) ai tah pay-ahj

What is causing this traffic jam?
Pourquoi y a-t-il un embouteillage?
poor-kwah ee-ah-teel ern an-boo-tery-ahj

What is the speed limit?
Quelle est la limitation de vitesse?
kail ai lah lee-mee-tah-syon der vee-tais

When is the rush hour?
Quelles sont les heures de pointe?
kail son lay zerr der pwant

Parking

When will the road be clear?
Quand est-ce que la voie sera dégagée?
kan es ker lah vwah ser-ra day-gah-jay

Do I need snow chains?
Est-ce que j'ai besoin de chaînes?
ais ker jay ber-zwern der shain

Parking

Can I park here?
Puis-je me garer là?
pwee-jer mer gah-ray lah

Do I need a parking disc?
Ai-je besoin d'un disque de stationnement?
ai-jer ber-zwern dern deesk der stah-syonn-man

Do I need coins for the meter?
Faut-il mettre des pièces dans le parcmètre?
foh-teel maitr day pyais dan ler pahrk-maitr

Do I need parking lights?
Faut-il laisser les feux de position allumés?
foh-teel lai-say lay fer der poh-zee-syon ah-lew-may

How long can I stay here?
Combien de temps puis-je stationner ici?
kohm-byern der tan pwee-jer stah-syonn-ay ee-see

Is it safe to park here?
Peut-on se garer ici sans risque?
per-ton ser gah-ray ee-see san reesk

What time does the car park close?
A quelle heure ferme le parking?
ah kail err fairm ler pahr-keeng

Where can I get a parking disc?
Où peut-on acheter un disque de stationnement?
oo per-ton ahsh-tay ern deesk der stah-syonn-man

Is there a car park?
Est-ce qu'il y a un parking?
ais keel-yah ern pahr-keeng

At the service station

Fill the tank, please
Le plein, s'il vous plaît
ler plern, seel voo play

— 25 litres of 3 star
— 25 litres de super
— *vernt-sank leetr der sew-pair*

— 25 litres of 4 star
— 25 litres de super-plus
— *vernt-sank leetr der sew-pair-plews*

At the service station

— 25 litres of diesel
— 25 (vingt cinq) litres de gazole
— *vernt-sank leetr der gah-zohl*

— 25 litres of unleaded petrol
— 25 (vingt cinq) litres de sans plomb
— *vernt-sank leetr der san plohm*

Can you clean the windscreen?
Nettoyez le pare-brise, s'il vous plaît
nai-twah-yay ler pahr-breez, seel voo play

   Check — the oil, please
   Vérifiez — l'huile, s'il vous plaît
vay-ree-fyay— lweel, seel voo play

      — the water, please
      — l'eau, s'il vous plaît
      — *loh, seel voo play*

      — the tyre pressure, please
      — les pneus, s'il vous plaît
      — *lay pner, seel voo play*

The pressure should be 2.3 at the front and 2.5 at the rear
C'est 2,3 (deux virgule trois) à l'avant et 2,5 (deux virgule cinq) à l'arrière
sai der veer-gewl trwah ah lah-van ay der veer-gewl sank ah lah-ryair

Do you take credit cards?
Acceptez-vous les cartes de crédit?
ahk-saip-tay voo lay kahrt der kray-dee

Breakdowns and repairs

Can you give me a can of petrol, please?
Avez-vous un bidon d'essence, s'il vous plaît?
ah-vay voo zern bee-don dai-sans, seel voo play

Can you give me — a push?
Pouvez-vous — me pousser?
poo-vay voo — mer poo-say

— a tow?
— me prendre en remorque?
— mer prandr an rer-mohrk

Can you send a recovery truck?
Pouvez-vous envoyer une dépanneuse?
poo-vay voo zan-vwah-yay ewn day-pah-nurz

Can you take me to the nearest garage?
Pouvez-vous me conduire au garage le plus proche?
poo-vay voo mer kohn-dweer oh gah-rahj ler plew prohsh

I have run out of petrol
Je suis en panne sèche
jer swee zan pahn saish

Breakdowns and repairs

Is there a telephone nearby?
Y a-t-il un téléphone près d'ici?
ee-ah-teel ern tay-lay-fohn prai dee-see

Do you have an emergency fan belt?
Avez-vous une courroie de secours?
ah-vay voo zewn koo-rwah der ser-koor

Do you have jump leads?
Avez-vous un câble de démarrage?
ah-vay voo zan kahbl der day-mah-rahj

I have a flat tyre
J'ai un pneu crevé
jay ern pner krer-vay

I have blown a fuse
Un fusible a sauté
ern few-zeebl ah soh-tay

I have locked myself out of the car
Les clefs sont enfermées à l'intérieur
lay klay son tan-fair-may zah lan-tay-ryerr

I have locked the ignition key inside the car
La clef de contact est enfermée à l'intérieur
lah klay der kohn-tahkt ai tan-fair-may ah lan-tay-ryerr

I have lost my key
J'ai perdu ma clef
jay pair-dew mah klay

Breakdowns and repairs

I need a new fan belt
Il me faut une courroie de ventilateur neuve
eel mer foh tewn koo-rwah der van-tee-lah-terr nerv

I think there is a bad connection
Je crois qu'il y a un mauvais contact
jer krwah keel yah ern moh-vai kohn-tahkt

Can you repair a flat tyre?
Pouvez-vous réparer un pneu crevé?
poo-vay voo ray-pah-ray ern pner krer-vay

My car — has been towed away
Ma voiture — a été emmenée à la fourrière
mah vwah-tewr — ah ay-tay an-mer-nay ah lah foo-ryair

— has broken down
— est en panne
— ai tan pahn

— will not start
— ne démarre pas
— ner day-mahr pah

My windscreen has cracked
Mon pare-brise est fêlé.
mon pahr-breez ai fai-lay

The air-conditioning does not work
La climatisation ne marche pas
lah klee-mah-tee-zah-syon ner mahrsh pah

Breakdowns and repairs

The battery is flat
Les accus sont à plat
lay zah-kew son tah plah

The engine has broken down
Le moteur est en panne
ler moh-terr ai tan pahn

The engine is overheating
Le moteur chauffe
ler moh-terr shohf

The exhaust pipe has fallen off
J'ai perdu mon pot d'échappement
jay pair-dew mon poh day-shahp-man

There is a leak in the radiator
Il y a une fuite au radiateur
eel yah ewn fweet oh rah-dyah-terr

Can you replace the windscreen wiper blades?
Pouvez-vous changer les balais des essuie-glace?
poo-vay voo shan-jay lay bah-lay day zai-swee-glahs

There is something wrong
Il y a un problème
eel yah an proh-blaim

There is something wrong with the car
La voiture ne marche pas
lah vwah-tewr ner mahrsh pah

Accidents and the police

Is there a mechanic here?
Y a-t-il un mécanicien?
ee-ah-teel ern may-kah-nee-syern

Can you find out what the trouble is?
Savez-vous ce qui ne va pas?
sah-vay voo ser kee ner vah pah

Do you have the spare parts?
Avez-vous les pièces détachées?
ah-vay voo lay pyais day-tah-shay

Is it serious?
Est-ce grave?
ais grahv

Can you repair it for the time being?
Pouvez-vous faire une réparation temporaire?
poo-vay voo fair ewn ray-pah-rah-syon tan-poh-rair

Will it take long to repair it?
Combien de temps faudra-t-il pour les réparations?
kohm-byern der tan foh-drah-teel poor lay ray-pah-rah-syon

Accidents and the police

There has been an accident
Il y a eu un accident
eel ya ew ern ahk-see-dan

Accidents and the police

We must call an ambulance
Il faut appeler une ambulance
eel foh tah-play ewn an-bew-lans

We must call the police
Il faut appeler la police
eel foh tah-play lah poh-lees

What is your name and address?
Quel est votre nom et votre adresse?
kail ai vohtr nohm ay vohtr ah-drais

You must not move
Ne bougez pas
ner boo-jay pah

He did not stop
Il ne s'est pas arrêté
eel ner sai pah zah-rai-tay

He is a witness
Il est témoin
eel ai tay-mwan

He overtook on a bend
Il a doublé dans un virage
eel ah doo-blay dan zern vee-rahj

He ran into the back of my car
Il m'a embouti à l'arrière
eel mah an-boo-tee ah lah-ryair

Accidents and the police

He stopped suddenly
Il s'est arrêté brusquement
eel sai tah-rai-tay brewsk-man

He was moving too fast
Il roulait trop vite
eel roo-lay troh veet

Here are my insurance documents
Voici mes pièces d'assurance
vwah-see may pyais dah-sew-rans

Here is my driving licence
Voici mon permis de conduire
vwah-see mon pair-mee der kon-dweer

How much is the fine?
Quel est le montant de la contravention?
kail ai ler mon-tan der lah kon-trah-van-syon

I have not got enough money. Can I pay at the police station?
Je n'ai pas assez d'argent. Puis-je payer au commissariat de police?
jer nay pah ah-say dahr-jan. pweej pay-yay oh koh-mee-sah-ryah der poh-lees

I am very sorry. I am a visitor
Je suis désolé. Je suis de passage
jer swee day-soh-lay. jer swee der pah-sahj

Accidents and the police

I did not know about the speed limit
Je ne savais pas que la vitesse était limitée
jer ner sah-vay pah ker lah vee-tais ay-tay lee-mee-tay

I did not understand the sign
Je n'ai pas compris le panneau
jer nay pah kohm-pree ler pah-noh

I did not see the sign
Je n'ai pas vu le panneau
jer nay pah vew ler pah-noh

I did not see the bicycle
Je n'ai pas vu la bicyclette
jer nay pah vew lah bee-see-klait

I could not stop in time
Je n'ai pas pu m'arrêter à temps
jer nay pah pew mah-rai-tay ah tan

I have not had anything to drink
Je n'ai rien bu
jer nay ryern bew

I was only driving at 50 km/h
Je ne roulais qu'à 50 km/h (cinquante kilomètre à l'heure)
jer ner roo-lay kah san-kant kee-loh-maitr ah lerr

I was overtaking
J'étais en train de dépasser
jay-tay an trern der day-pah-say

I was parking
J'étais en train de me garer
jay-tay an trern der mer gah-ray

That car was too close
La voiture me suivait de trop près
lah vwah-tewr mer swee-vay der troh prai

The brakes failed
Les freins ont lâché
lay frern zon lah-shay

The car number (licence number) was...
Le numéro d'immatriculation était...
ler new-may-roh dee-mah-tree-kew-lah-syon ay-tay...

The car skidded
La voiture a dérapé
lah vwah-tewr ah day-rah-pay

The car swerved
La voiture a fait un écart
lah vwah-tewr ah fai tan ay-kahr

The car turned right without signalling
La voiture a tourné à droite sans prévenir
lah vwah-tewr ah toor-nay ah drwaht san pray-ver-neer

The road was icy
La route était verglacée
lah root ay-tay vair-glah-say

Car parts

The tyre burst
Le pneu a éclaté
ler pner ah ay-klah-tay

Car parts

accelerator
accélérateur
ahk-say-lay-rah-terr

aerial
antenne
an-tain

air filter
filtre à air
feeltr ah air

alternator
alternateur
ahl-tair-nah-terr

antifreeze
antigel
an-tee-jail

automatic
automatique
oh-toh-mah-teek

axle
essieu
ai-syer

battery
accus
ah-kew

bonnet
capot
kah-poh

boot
coffre
kohfr

brake fluid
liquide de frein
lee-keed de frern

brakes
freins
frern

bulb
ampoule
an-pool

bumper
pare-chocs
pahr-shohk

carburettor
carburateur
kahr-bew-rah-terr

child seat
siège pour enfant
syaij poor an-fan

choke
starter
stahr-tair

clutch
embrayage
an-brai-yaj

cylinder
cylindre
see-lerndr

disc brake
freins à disques
frern ah deesk

distributor
delco
dail-koh

door
portière
pohr-tyair

dynamo
dynamo
dee-nah-moh

electrical system
circuit électrique
seer-kwee ay-laik-treek

engine
moteur
moh-terr

exhaust system
échappement
ay-shahp-man

fan belt
courroie de ventilateur
koo-rwah der van-tee-lah-terr

foot pump
pompe à pied
pohmp ah pyay

Car parts

fuel gauge
jauge d'essence
johj dai-sans

fuel pump
pompe d'alimentation
pohmp dah-lee-man-tah-syon

fuse
fusible
few-seebl

gear box
boîte de vitesses
bwaht der vee-tais

gear lever
levier de vitesses
lai-vyay der vee-tais

generator
génératrice
jay-nay-rah-trees

hammer
marteau
mahr-toh

hand brake
frein à main
frern ah mern

hazard lights
feux de détresse
fer der day-trais

headlights
phares
fahr

heating system
chauffage
shoh-fahj

hood
capote
kah-poht

horn
klaxon
klahk-son

hose
tuyau
tew-yoh

ignition
allumage
ah-lew-mahj

ignition key
clef de contact
klay der kon-tahkt

indicator
clignotant
kleen-yoh-tan

jack
cric
kreek

lights
feux
fer

lock
dispositif antivol
dees-poh-see-teef an-tee-vohl

oil filter
filtre à huile
feeltr ah weel

oil
huile
weel

oil pressure
pression d'huile
prai-syon dweel

petrol
essence
ai-sans

points
vis platinées
vees plah-tee-nay

pump
pompe
pohmp

radiator
radiateur
rah-dyah-terr

rear view mirror
rétroviseur
ray-troh-vee-serr

reflectors
réflecteurs
ray-flaik-terr

reversing light
feux de recul
fer der rer-kewl

roof-rack
galerie
gah-ler-ree

screwdriver
tournevis
toorn-vees

Car parts

seat belt
ceinture de sécurité
sern-tewr der say-kew-ree-tay

seat
siège
see-aij

shock absorber
amortisseur
ah-mohr-tee-serr

silencer
silencieux
see-lan-syer

socket set
prise
preez

spanner
clef anglaise
klay an-glayz

spare part
pièce détachée
pyais day-tah-shay

spark plug
bougie
boo-jee

speedometer
compteur
kohmp-terr

starter motor
démarreur
day-mah-rerr

steering
direction
dee-raik-syon

steering wheel
volant
voh-lan

stoplight
feu rouge
fer rooj

sun roof
toit ouvrant
twa toov-ran

suspension
suspension
sews-pan-syon

tools
outils
oo-tee

towbar
barre de remorquage
bahr der rer-mohr-kahj

transmission
transmission
trans-mee-syon

trunk
coffre
kohfr

tyre
pneu
pner

tyre pressure
pression des pneus
prai-syon day pner

warning light
voyant lumineux
voh-yan lew-mee-ner

water
eau
oh

wheel
roue
roo

windscreen
pare-brise
pahr-breez

wipers
essuie-glace
ais-wee-glahs

wrench
clef anglaise
klay an-glayz

EATING OUT

Good value and good quality

Eating out is a national pastime for the French. Even small towns have at least one ambitious restaurant, and, by British standards, restaurant meals are excellent value. The emphasis is on fresh local produce and even the humblest, dowdiest-looking place may produce food of surprisingly good quality.

Meals and menus

Proper restaurants and hotel dining rooms (other than in the major cities) stick to pretty rigid hours, and meals are generally served earlier than in Britain. Lunch (*le déjeuner*) – traditionally a leisurely two-hour affair – is the main meal of the day. Popular restaurants start filling up soon after noon. Book ahead for Sunday lunch. Dinner (*le dîner*) is usually served from around 7pm or 7.30pm until 8.30pm or 9pm; in some areas it's difficult to get dinner after 8pm.

Cafés (and brasseries – larger and smarter) are usually open all day for snacks or more substantial meals, and are useful if you haven't time to linger over a three-course meal. Prices in fashionable places – particularly in Paris – are very high, though you can stay for as long as you like for the price of one drink.

The word 'menu' has a more precise meaning in France than in Britain: it means a meal consisting of several courses with a narrow choice of dishes, at a fixed all-in price. Most restaurants offer several such menus at a range of prices, and may or may not also offer a wider choice of individual dishes from *la carte*. Menus invariably offer better value. The English expression 'à la carte menu' is a contradiction in terms in France.

The French way

- meals are not meant to be rushed, so service may seem slow
- waiters aren't called *garçon* – use *monsieur, madame* or *mademoiselle*
- the French don't drink coffee or tea during meals
- a simple restaurant will expect you to use the same knife and fork throughout the meal
- you will automatically be given bread with your meal but not a side plate or butter
- vegetables are often served separately from the meat, salads invariably so
- meat is normally served very rare or *saignant;* if you want it practically raw, ask for it *bleu;* if you want it rare, ask for it *à point,* for medium *bien cuit*
- cheese comes before dessert

Food

Even if France had no other attractions for the visitor, the country would retain the loyalty of many British fans because of its food. The French attitude to food is quite different from that of the British – put simply, they care about it.

Serious students of French food identify different styles of cooking – in particular *haute cuisine,* the rich, expensive fare traditionally associated with top-notch restaurants, and *nouvelle cuisine,* the modern version, using much less cream and butter.

Styles of cooking and sauces

Alsacienne (à l') — usually with sauerkraut, ham and sausages

Armoricaine (à l') — with sauce of tomatoes, herbs, white wine, brandy

Anglaise (à l') — plain, boiled

ballotine — boned, stuffed and rolled into a bundle

Béarnaise — sauce flavoured with tarragon and vinegar

Bercy — sauce with wine, shallots and bone marrow

Berrichonne (à la) — with bacon, cabbage, onions and chestnuts

beurre blanc — butter sauce with shallots and dry wine or vinegar

Styles of cooking and sauces

beurre noir — browned butter with vinegar

bigarade — bitter orange sauce

bonne femme — poached in white wine with onions and mushrooms

Bordelaise — sauce of red wine and bone marrow

boulangère (à la) — braised or baked with onions and potatoes

bourgeoise (à la) — with carrots, onions and bacon

Bourguignonne (à la) — cooked with burgundy, onions and mushrooms

Bretonne (à la) — served with haricot beans, sometimes as a purée

cardinal — rich, red fish sauce with mushrooms, truffles (usually for lobster)

chasseur — with shallots, mushrooms, tomatoes

chemise(en) — wrapped, generally in pastry

confit(e) — preserved or candied

court-bouillon — aromatic poaching liquid

croûte (en) — pastry case (in a)

daube — meat slowly braised in wine and herbs

diable — highly seasoned sauce; also type of cooking pot

Dijonnaise (à la) — with mustard sauce

farci(e) — stuffed

fourré (au) — filled

galantine — cold pressed poultry, meat or fish in jelly

Hollandaise — sauce with butter, egg yolk and lemon juice

Lyonnaise (à la) — with onions

Cheese

Normande (à la) — with cream and any or all of: calvados, cider, apples

Provençal (à la) — with tomatoes, oil and garlic

roulade (de) — roll (of)

rouille — strongly flavoured creamy sauce with fish soups

Cheese

Part of the fun of eating cheese in France is that there are always new varieties to discover and try out. 'Try anything once' should be your motto. Be prepared for lots of pleasant surprises, a huge variety of flavours from all over the country and methods of cheesemaking that are quite diverse are are often jealously guarded secrets. It is customary in France to eat the cheese course before the dessert. The cheeses will be served with bread but not butter. Wherever you are, be sure to sample the local produce.

Principal cheeses

You're likely to come across these major varieties of cheese anywhere in France.

Brie — Soft cheese always made in round discs, varying in size. A good one should be yellow, creamy but not runny. It is made by factories in Brie and other parts of France and often called by the name of the area where it is made, for example Brie de Meaux or Brie de Melun

bleu d'Auvergne — Blue mould cheese created by a 19th-century peasant

Camembert — Small circular soft cheese invented in about 1790 by a farmer's wife, Mme Harel, whose statue you can see in the village of Camembert, near Vimoutiers in Normandy

Livarot — Soft, strong cheese with orange rind, from a small market town in Normandy

Munster — Large, round, supple cheese with orange rind, matured for three to six weeks, with strong smell and spicy flavour. Made in Alsace

Pont-l'Evêque — Small, square, pungent cheese, made from whole or skimmed milk

Port-Salut — Creamy, yellow, whole-milk cheese, first made at the Trappist Monastery of Port du Salut in Brittany

Reblochon — Soft, smooth cows' milk cheese from Savoie, with mild, creamy flavour

Roquefort — The true Roquefort, made in the little town of the same name in the Massif Central, is manufactured exclusively from ewes' milk. The unique feature of this cheese is that the curds are mixed with a special type of breadcrumb, causing a green mould to develop. The cheeses are stored in damp, cool caves for 30 or 40 days. Experts say it should then be left to ripen for a year

Regional cheeses

bleu de Bresse — Factory-made blue cheese from the

Cheese

Lyonnais in the shape of a small cylinder; creamy and smooth

Brillat-Savarin — Mild, creamy cheese from Normandy, named after the gastronome

Cantal — Hard, strong, yellow cheese, with a nutty flavour, made in the Auvergne

Chabichou — Small, cone-shaped goats' milk cheese, with strong smell and flavour; from the Poitou area

Chaource — White, soft and creamy cheese from Burgundy, made in cylinders

Dauphin — Soft, herb-seasoned cheese from Champagne Ardennes area, said to be named after Louis XIV's son

Epoisses — Soft, whole-milk cheese with spicy smell and flavour made all over Burgundy and central France

Olivet bleu — Small, rich, fruity cheese with bluish skin, sometimes wrapped in plane tree leaves: it comes from the Loire

Rollot — Cheese in the form of a disc with yellow rind, spicy smell and flavour

Saint-Marcellin — Small, round, mild cheese made of cow's milk from Savoie

Tomme — Name for a large number of cheeses, mainly from the Alps. Usually mild

Ste-Mauré — Soft creamy goats' milk cheese from Touraine

St-Nectaire — Flat, round cheese with mild but aromatic flavour, made on the Dordogne

Reservations

Should we reserve a table?
Faut-il réserver une table?
foh-teel ray-sair-vay ewn tahbl

Can I book a table for four at 8 o'clock?
Je voudrais réserver une table pour quatre pour huit heures
jer voo-dray ray-sair-vay ewn tahbl poor kahtr poor weet err

Can we have a table for four?
Une table pour quatre, s'il vous plaît
ewn tahbl poor kahtr, seel voo play

We would like a table — by the window
Nous voudrions une table — près de la fenêtre
noo voo-dryon ewn tahbl — prai der lah fer-naitr

— on the terrace
— sur la terrasse
— sewr lah tay-rahs

I am a vegetarian
Je suis végétarien
jer swee vay-jay-tah-ryern

Useful questions

Do you have a local speciality?
Avez-vous une spécialité régionale?
ah-vay voo zewn spay-syah-lee-tay ray-jyon-ahl

Do you have a set menu?
Avez-vous un menu à prix fixe?
ah-vay voo ern mer-new ah pree feeks

What do you recommend?
Que recommandez-vous?
ker rer-koh-man-day voo

What is the dish of the day?
Quel est le plat du jour?
kail ai ler plah dew joor

What is the soup of the day?
Quelle est la soupe du jour?
kail ai lah soop dew joor

What is this called?
Comment s'appelle ce plat?
koh-man sah-pail ser plah

What is this dish like?
Ce plat, il est comment?
ser plah, eel ai koh mon

126

Is this good?
Est-ce que c'est bon?
ais ker sai bon

Which local wine do you recommend?
Quel vin de pays recommandez-vous?
kail vern der payy rer-koh-man-day voo

Are vegetables included?
Est-ce que les légumes sont inclus?
ais ker lay lay-gewm son tern-klew

Is the local wine good?
Est-ce que le vin de pays est bon?
ais ker ler vern der payy ai bon

Is this cheese very strong?
Ce fromage, est-il très fort?
ser froh-mahj ai-teel trai fohr

How much is this?
C'est combien?
sai kohm-byern

Do you have yoghurt?
Avez-vous du yaourt?
ah-vay voo dew yah-oor

How do I eat this?
Comment mange-t-on cela?
koh-man manj-ton ser-lah

Ordering your meal

The menu, please
Le menu, s'il vous plaît
ler mer-new, seel voo play

Can we start with soup?
De la soupe pour commencer, s'il vous plaît
der lah soop poor koh-man-say, seel voo play

That is for me
C'est pour moi
sai poor mwah

Can we have some bread?
Du pain, s'il vous plaît
dew pern, seel voo play

Could we have some butter?
Du beurre, s'il vous plaît
dew berr, seel voo play

I will have salad
Je prendrai de la salade
jer pran-drai der lah sah-lahd

I will take that
Je prendrai ceci
jer pran-drai ser-see

Ordering your meal

I will take the set menu
Je prendrai le menu à prix fixe
jer pran-drai ler mer-new ah pree feeks

I like my steak — rare
J'aime mon steack — saignant
jaim mon staik — sai-nyan

— medium rare
— à point
— ah pwan

— very rare
— bleu
— bler

— well done
— bien cuit
— byern kwee

Could we have some more bread please?
Encore du pain, s'il vous plaît
an-kohr dew pern, seel voo play

Can I see the menu again, please?
Repassez-moi le menu, s'il vous plaît
rer-pah-say mwah ler mer-new, seel voo play

Wine

Wine is an integral part of French life. The vineyards of France produce a significant proportion of the world's wine, and the people of France consume much of that volume themselves. The choice of wines is enormous: everything from *vin ordinaire* in plastic bottles, costing no more than mineral water, to the cream of the crop from Bordeaux and Burgundy – the best wines in the world.

Unless you are very familiar with French wines, choosing from the wine list (*la carte des vins*) can be an intimidating experience. Some restaurants produce off-putting lists with pages of wines and prices that are very high indeed.

But if the big-name Bordeaux and Burgundy wines are out of reach, there are nearly always plenty of much cheaper alternatives, even in the top restaurants; many wines from the Loire and Rhone valleys or from the south and south-west are now finding their way on to wine lists throughout the country.

The house wine – *vin réserve du patron* or *vin de la maison* – is almost always a good bet: if it carries the restaurant's own label, it will usually have been carefully selected.

Reading a label

The ways in which wines are described on labels vary widely

Wine vocabulary

from region to region. Running across all the variations is a national system of identification employing four classifications.

Appellation (d'Origine) Contrôlée (AC or AOC) — A guarantee of origin and authenticity, applied to all major wines. An *appellation* may apply to a whole region (for example Bourgogne), a part of a region (for example Côtes de Nuit), a specific village (e.g. Gevrey-Chambertin) or even a particular vineyard (e.g. Grand Cru Clos de Bèze). In general, within a given region, the larger the geographic area described on the label, the cheaper and lesser quality the wine.

Vin Délimité de Qualité Supérieure (VDQS) — The second rank of *appellations* for regions producing minor wines. Some are of very good quality, being denied an AC only because they employ non-traditional grapes. As these better wines gain AC status, the VDQS label is being phased out.

Vin de Pays — 'Country wine' from a specific area – which may be a village or a whole region. Standards vary enormously.

Vin de Table or Vin Ordinaire — Blended wine, usually sold under a brand name.

Wine vocabulary

Blanc de blancs — White wine made from white grapes

Wine vocabulary

Cave — Cellar or any wine establishment

Cave coopérative — Wine growers' cooperative, often a very good place to taste and buy

Chai — Cellar at ground level, sometimes meaning a warehouse

Château — A wine-growing estate, with or without a grand house, particularly in the Bordeaux area

Clairet — Very light red wine

Claret — Traditional English term for red wine from Bordeaux

Clos — Prestigious vineyard, often walled, found particularly in Burgundy and Alsace

Côte(s)/côteaux — Hillsides, generally producing better wines than lower vineyards

Crémant — In Champagne, 'less sparkling'; elsewhere, high-quality sparkling wine made by the Champagne method

Cru (Growth) — A term used in classifying the wines of different vineyards. In Bordeaux there is an elaborate and confusing system of *crus*, rooted firmly in the 19th century and not an entirely useful guide to quality. In Burgundy and Champagne, *Grand Cru* indicates the most prestigious wines, *Premier Cru* the second rank

Cuve Close — Method of making sparkling wine, generally inferior to the Champagne method

Cuvée du patron — House wine

Domaine — A wine estate, particularly in Burgundy

Ordering drinks

Méthode champenoise — Sparkling wine made by the Champagne method

Mise (en bouteille) au château/à la propriété/au domaine — Bottled on the wine-maker's premises; usually a good thing

Moelleux — Mellow, sweet

Mousseux — Sparkling

Négociant — Wine merchant

Perlant/perlé — Very slightly sparkling

Pétillant — Slightly sparkling

Primeur — Young wine

Propriétaire-Récoltant — Owner-manager

Récolte — Crop

Réserve de la maison/du patron— House wine in a restaurant

Vendange tardive — Late vintage, especially in Alsace – the grapes are picked only when they have reached a certain sweetness

Vignoble — Vineyard

Viticulteur — Vine-grower

Ordering drinks

The wine list, please
La carte des vins, s'il vous plaît
lah kahrt day vern, seel voo play

Ordering drinks

A bottle of house red wine, please
Une bouteille de la cuvée du patron, s'il vous plaît
ewn boo-tery der lah kew-vay dew pah-tron, seel voo play

A glass of dry white wine, please
Un verre de vin blanc, s'il vous plaît
ern vair der vern blan, seel voo play

Another bottle of red wine, please
Une autre bouteille de vin rouge, s'il vous plaît
ewn ohtr boo-tery der vern rooj, seel voo play

Another glass, please
Un autre verre, s'il vous plaît
ern ohtr vair, seel voo play

We will take the beaujolais
Nous prendrons le beaujolais
noo pran-dron ler boh-joh-lay

Two beers, please
Deux bières, s'il vous plaît
der byair, seel voo play

Some plain water, please
De l'eau du robinet, s'il vous plaît
der loh dew roh-bee-nay, seel voo play

Can we have some mineral water?
De l'eau minérale, s'il vous plaît
der loh mee-nay-rahl, seel voo play

Black coffee, please
Un café (noir), s'il vous plaît
ern kah-fay (nwahr), seel voo play

Coffee with milk, please
Un café-crème, s'il vous plaît
ern kah-fay kraim, seel voo play

Tea with milk, please
Un thé au lait, s'il vous plaît
ern tay oh lay, seel voo play

Paying the bill

What is the total?
Ça fait combien en tout?
sah fai kohm-byern an too

Do you accept traveller's cheques?
Acceptez-vous les chèques de voyage?
ahk-saip-tay voo lay shaik der vohy-ahj

I would like to pay with my credit card
Je voudrais payer avec ma carte de crédit
jer voo-dray pay-yay ah-vaik mah kahrt der kray-dee

Is there any extra charge?
Y a-t-il un supplément?
ee-ah-teel ern sew-play-man

Paying the bill

Is service included?
Est-ce que le service est compris?
ais ker ler sair-vees ai kohm-pree

Can I have a receipt?
Puis-je avoir un reçu?
pwee-jer ah-vwahr ern rer-sew?

Can I have an itemised bill?
Puis-je avoir une note détaillée?
pwee-jer ah-vwahr ewn nawt day-tah-yay

You have given me the wrong change
Vous vous êtes trompé en me rendant monnaie
voo voo zait trohm-pay an mer ran-dan moh-nay

This is not correct
C'est inexact
sai tee-naig-sahkt

This is not my bill
C'est addition n'est pas à moi
sait ahdee-syan nay paz ah mwa

I do not have enough currency
Je n'ai pas assez de liquide
jer nay pah ah-say der lee-keed

I do not have enough money
Je n'ai pas assez d'argent
jer nay pah ah-say dahr-jan

Complaints and compliments

Waiter! We have been waiting for a long time
Monsieur/Madame/Mademoiselle! Nous attendons depuis
   longtemps
*mer-syer/ma-dam/mad-mwa-zel noo zah-tan-don der-pwee
   lon-tan*

This is cold
C'est froid
sai frwah

This is not what I ordered
Ce n'est pas ce que j'ai commandé
ser nai pah ser ker jay koh-man-day

Can I have the recipe?
Puis-je avoir la recette?
pwee-jer ah-vwahr lah rer-sait

This is excellent
C'est délicieux
sai day-lee-syer

The meal was excellent
Le repas était délicieux
ler rer-pah ay-tai day-lee-syer

137

Menu reader

abricots
ahb-ree-koh
apricots

ail
ah-ee
garlic

ananas
ah-nah-nah
pineapple

artichaut
ahr-tee-shoh
artichoke

asperge
ahs-pairj
asparagus

aubergine
oh-bair-jeen
aubergine

aubergines farcies
oh-bair-jeen fahr-see
stuffed aubergines

avocat
ah-voh-kah
avocado

bananes
bah-nahn
bananas

basilic
bah-see-leek
basil

beignets
bay-nyay
doughnuts, fritters

betterave
bait-rahv
beetroot

beurre
berr
butter

bifteck
beef-taik
beefsteak

blanquette de veau
blan-kait der voh
veal in white sauce

boeuf bourguignon
berf boor-gee-nyon
beef stewed in red wine

boeuf braisé
berf bray-zay
braised beef

boeuf en daube
berf an dohb
beef stew

bouillabaisse
boo-yah-bais
spicy fish soup with garlic

bouillon de boeuf
boo-yon der berf
beef broth

bouillon de poulet
boo-yon der poo-lay
chicken broth

calmar
kahl-mahr
squid

canard
kah-nahr
duck

canard à l'orange
kah-nahr ah loh-ranj
duck with orange

carottes
kah-roht
carrots

cassis
kah-see
blackcurrants

céleri
say-lai-ree
celery

cerfeuil
sair-fery
chervil

cerises
ser-reez
cherries

champignons
shan-pee-nyon
mushrooms

139

Menu reader

champignons à l'ail
shan-peen-yon ah lah-ee
mushrooms with garlic

champignons en sauce
shan-peen-yon an sohs
mushrooms in sauce

chicorée
shee-koh-ray
chicory, endive

chou
shoo
cabbage

choucroute
shoo-kroot
sauerkraut

chou-fleur
shoo-fler
cauliflower

choux de Bruxelles
shoo der brew-sail
Brussels sprouts

ciboulette
see-boo-lait
chives

citron
see-tron
lemon

civet de lapin
see-vay der lah-pern
rabbit stew

compote de pommes
kohm-poht der pohm
apple compote

concombre
kon-kohmbr
cucumber

confiture
kon-fee-tewr
jam

coq au vin
kohk oh vern
coq au vin

cornichon
kohr-nee-shon
gherkin

côtelette d'agneau
koht-lait dahn-yoh
lamb cutlet

côtelette de porc
koht-lait der pohr
pork cutlet

côtelette de veau
koht-lait der voh
veal cutlet

côtelette grillée
koht-lait gree-yay
grilled cutlet

coulis de pommes
koo-lee der pohm
apple sauce

courge
koorj
squash

courgettes
koor-jait
courgettes

crème anglaise
kraim an-glayz
custard

crème caramel
kraim kah-rah-mail
caramel custard

cresson
krai-son
watercress

crêpes
kraip
thin pancakes

— à la confiture
— ah lah kon-fee-tewr
— with jam

— au chocolat
— oh shoh-koh-lah
— with chocolate

croque-monsieur
krohk-mer-syer
cheese and ham toasted
sandwich

cuisses de grenouilles
kwees der grer-nooy
frogs' legs

dattes
daht
dates

141

Menu reader

dessert
day-sair
pudding

dinde
dernd
turkey

échalottes
ay-shah-loht
shallots

en sauce
an sohs
in sauce

épinards
ay-pee-nahr
spinach

estragon
ais-trah-gon
tarragon

faisan
fay-san
pheasant

feuille de laurier
fery der loh-ryay
bayleaf

fèves
faiv
broad beans

filet de boeuf
fee-lay der berf
steak fillet

filet de colin
fee-lay der koh-lern
hake fillet

flan au fromage blanc
flan oh froh-mahj blan
cheesecake

fondue savoyarde
fon-dew sah-voh-yahrd
cheese fondue

fraises
fraiz
strawberries

fraises à la crème fraîche
fraiz ah lah kraim fraish
strawberries with cream

framboises
fran-bwahz
raspberries

frites
freet
French fries/chips

fruits à la crème fouettée
frwee zah lah kraim fwai-tay
fruit with whipped cream

gâteau
gah-toh
cake

gâteau aux amandes
gah-toh oh zah-mand
almond cake

gâteau de riz
gah-toh der ree
rice pudding

gâteau de Savoie
gah-toh der sah-vwah
sponge cake

gigot d'agneau
jee-goh dahn-yoh
roast leg of lamb

glace
glahs
ice cream

grenades
grer-nahd
pomegranates

grillé/au feu de bois
gree-yay/oh fer der bwah
grilled/barbecued

hachis parmentier
ahshee pahr-man-tyay
shepherd's pie

haricots blancs
ah-ree-koh blan
haricot beans

haricots verts
ah-ree-koh vair
French beans

homard
oh-mahr
lobster

huile
weel
oil

huîtres
weetr
oysters

Menu reader

jambon fumé
jan-bon few-may
cured ham

jardinière de légumes
jahr-dee-nyair der lay-gewm
diced vegetables

jarret (d'agneau, etc)
jah-ray (dahn-yoh)
shank (of lamb etc)

laitue
lay-tew
lettuce

langouste
lan-goost
crayfish

langue
lang
tongue

lapin farci
lah-pern fahr-see
stuffed rabbit

légumes
lay-gewm
vegetables

maïs
mah-ees
sweet corn

maquereau
mahk-roh
mackerel

maquereau
mahk-roh
mackerel

melon
mer-lon
melon

menthe
mant
mint

meringue au citron
may-rerng oh see-tron
lemon meringue

moules
mool
mussels

mousse au chocolat
moos oh shoh-koh-lah
chocolate mousse

moules frites
mool freet
mussels and French fries

moules marinières
mool mah-ree-nyair
mussels in wine and garlic

navet
nah-vay
turnip

oeuf à la coque
erf ah lah kohk
soft boiled egg

oeufs au bacon
er zoh bah-kon
eggs with bacon

oeufs au jambon
er zoh jan-bon
eggs with ham

oeufs au plat
er zoh plah
fried eggs

oeufs brouillés
er brwee-yay
scrambled eggs

oie
wah
goose

oignons
wahn-yon
onions

olives
oh-leev
olives

oranges
oh-ranj
oranges

palourdes
pah-loord
clams

pamplemousse
panp-moos
grapefruit

panais
pah-nai
parsnip

pastèque
pahs-taik
watermelon

Menu reader

pâtes
paht
pasta

pâtes aux oeufs
paht oh zer
egg noodles

pêche
paish
peach

persil
pair-seel
parsley

petits pains
per-tee pern
bread rolls

petits pois
per-tee pwah
sweet, young peas

poire
pwahr
pear

poireaux
pwah-roh
leeks

poisson
pwah-son
fish

poisson mariné
pwah-son mah-ree-nay
marinated fish

poivron rouge
pwahv-ron rooj
red pepper

poivron vert
pwahv-ron vair
green pepper

pomme au four
pohm oh foor
roast apple

pommes
pohm
apples

pommes de terre dauphinoises
pohm der tair doh-fee-nwahz
sliced potatoes baked with cream and cheese

pommes rôties
pohm roh-tee
roast potatoes

potage aux champignons
poh-tahj oh shan-pee-nyon
cream of mushroom soup

potage aux haricots rouges
poh-tahj oh zah-ree-koh rooj
kidney-bean soup

potage aux poireaux
poh-tahj oh pwah-roh
leek soup

potage aux pois
poh-tahj oh pwah
pea soup

potage aux tomates
poh-tahj oh toh-maht
tomato soup

potage de légumes
poh-tahj der lay-gewm
cream of vegetable soup

potage de poulet
poh-tahj der poo-lay
chicken soup

poulet frit/pané
poo-lay freet/pah-nay
fried/breaded chicken

poulet rôti
poo-lay roh-tee
baked/roasted chicken

prunes
prewn
plums

purée de pommes de terre
pew-ray der pohm der tair
mashed potatoes

radis
rah-dee
radishes

ragoût de boeuf
rah-goo der berf
beef stew

ragoût de poulet
rah-goo der poo-lay
chicken stew

raisins
rai-zern
grapes

Menu reader

reines-claude
rain-klohd
greengages

rillettes
reel-ait
potted meat

rognons en sauce
roh-nyon an sohs
stewed kidney

romarin
roh-mah-rern
rosemary

rôti de porc
roh-tee der pohr
roast pork

rouget
roo-jay
mullet

salade
sah-lahd
salad

salade composée
sah-lahd kohm-poh-say
mixed salad

salade de concombre
sah-lahd der kon-kohmbr
cucumber salad

salade de fruits
sah-lahd der frwee
fruit salad

salade de maïs
sah-lahd der mah-ees
corn salad

salade de pommes de terre
sah-lahd der pohm der tair
potato salad

salade de tomates
sah-lahd der toh-maht
tomato salad

salade russe
sah-lahd rews
Russian salad

sandwich au jambon
san-weesh oh jan-bon
ham sandwich

sardines
sahr-deen
sardines

sauce à l'oignon
sohs ah loh-nyon
onion sauce

sauce au vin
sohs oh vern
wine sauce

sauce aux poivrons verts
sohs oh pwahv-ron vair
green pepper sauce

sauce tomate
sohs toh-maht
tomato sauce

saucisse
soh-sees
sausage

sauge
sohj
sage

scampi
skahm-pee
scampi

seiche
saish
cuttlefish

sole meunière
sohl mer-nyair
sole in butter with parsley

steack au poivre
staik oh pwahvr
pepper steak

steack frites
staik freet
steak and French fries

tarte
tahrt
pie

tarte aux pommes
tahrt oh pohm
apple tart

thon
ton
tuna

thym
tern
thyme

tomates
toh-maht
tomatoes

Drinks

tripes
treep
tripe

truite
trweet
trout

truite au beurre
trweet oh berr
fried trout

truite grillée
trweet gree-yay
grilled trout

viande
vee-and
meat

viande grillée
vee-and gree-yay
grilled meat

vinaigre
vee-naigr
vinegar

wiener schnitzel (escalope
de veau panée)
ais-kah-lohp der voh pah-nay
veal escalope

yaourt
yah-oor
yoghurt

Drinks

armagnac
ahr-mahn-yahk
armagnac

bière
byair
beer

bière brune
byair brewn
stout

bière en boîte
byair an bwaht
canned beer

bière en canette
byair an kah-nait
bottled beer

café
kah-fay
black coffee

café au lait
kah-fay oh lay
coffee with milk (breakfast)

café crème
kah-fay kraim
coffee with steamed milk

café glacé
kah-fay glah-say
iced coffee

café irlandais
kah-fay eer-lan-day
Irish coffee

café soluble
kah-fay soh-lewb
instant coffee

calvados
kahl-vah-dohs
apple brandy

camomille
kah-moh-meel
camomile tea

champagne
shan-pah-nyer
champagne

cidre
seedr
cider

coca-cola
koh-kah-koh-lah
coke

cognac
kohn-yahk
brandy

déca
day-kah
decaffeinated coffee

eau minérale
oh mee-nay-rahl
mineral water

express
aiks-prais
expresso coffee

Drinks

jus d'orange
jew doh-ranj
orange juice

jus de pomme
jew der pohm
apple juice

jus de raisin
jew der rai-zern
grape juice

kir
keer
blackcurrant liqueur

kirsch
keersh
cherry brandy

limonade
lee-moh-nahd
lemonade

liqueur
lee-kerr
liqueur

nectar d'abricot
naik-tahr dah-bree-koh
apricot juice

nectar de pêche
naik-tahr der paish
peach juice

orangeade
oh-ran-jahd
orange drink

pastis
pahs-tee
aniseed spirit

rhum
ron
rum

sangria
sahn-gree-ah
sangria

Schweppes
shwaips
tonic water

soda
soh-dah
soda

thé au lait
tay oh lay
tea with milk

thé citron
tay see-tron
lemon tea

un cognac
an koh-nyahk
a brandy

un (verre de) vin blanc
ern vair der vern blan
a glass of white wine

un (verre de) vin rouge
ern vair der vern rooj
a glass of red wine

une bière
ewn byair
a large beer

vin rosé
vern roh-zay
rosé wine

whisky
wees-kee
whisky

Out and About

The weather

The climate of France is not generally the main reason why people visit the country – unless they have chosen a skiing holiday. The climate of northern France is not unlike our own and is prone to rain and unpredictable changes. The centre, east and south of France have warmer climates, while the west coast is cooled by its proximity to the Atlantic Ocean.

Isn't it a lovely day?
Belle journée, n'est-ce pas?
bail joor-nay, nais pah

Is it going to get any warmer?
Est-ce qu'il va faire plus chaud?
ais keel vah fair plew shoh

Is it going to stay like this?
Est-ce que ce temps va durer?
ais ker ser tan vah dew-ray

Is there going to be a thunderstorm?
Va-t-il y avoir un orage?
vah-teel ee ah-vwahr ern oh-rahj

It has stopped snowing
Il ne neige plus
eel ner naij plew

There is a cool breeze
Il y a un vent frais
eel yah ern van frai

What is the temperature?
Quelle est la température?
kail ai lah tan-pay-rah-tewr

Will the weather improve?
Est-ce que le temps va s'arranger?
ais ker ler tan vah sah-ran-jay

It is far too hot
Il fait beaucoup trop chaud
eel fai boh-koo troh shoh

It is foggy
Il y a du brouillard
eel yah dew brwee-yahr

It is going to be fine
Il va   faire beau
eel vah fair boh

It is going to be windy
Il va faire du vent
eel vah fair dew van

On the beach

It is going to rain
Il va pleuvoir
eel vah pler-vwahr

It is going to snow
Il va neiger
eel vah nai-jay

It is raining again
Il pleut de nouveau
eel pler der noo-voh

It is very cold
Il fait très froid
eel fai trai frwah

It is very windy
Il y a beaucoup de vent
eel yah boh-koo der van

Will the wind die down?
Est-ce que le vent va tomber?
ais-ker ler van vah tohm-bay

On the beach

Can you recommend a quiet beach?
Pouvez-vous nous recommander une plage tranquille?
poo-vay voo noo rer-koh-man-day ewn plahj tran-keel

Is it safe to swim here?
Peut-on se baigner ici sans danger?
per-ton ser bain-yay ee-see san dan-jay

Is the current strong?
Est-ce que le courant est fort?
ais kerler koo-ran ai fohr

Is the sea calm?
Est-ce que la mer est calme?
ais ker lah mair ai kahlm

Is there a lifeguard here?
Y a-t-il un maître nageur?
ee-ah-teel an maitr nah-jerr

Is this beach private?
Est-ce que la plage est privée?
ais ker lah plahj ai pree-vay

When is — high tide?
A quelle heure est — la marée haute?
ah kail err ai — lah mah-ree oht

— low tide?
— la marée basse?
— lah mah-ree bahs

Can I rent — a sailing boat?
Puis-je louer — un voilier?
pweej loo-ay — ern vwah-lyay

157

Sport and recreation

Can I rent — a rowing boat?
Puis-je louer — une barque?
pweej loo-ay — ewn bahrk

Is it possible to go — sailing?
Peut-on faire — de la voile?
per-ton fair — der lah vwahl

— surfing?
— du surf?
— dew sewrf

— water skiing?
— du ski nautique?
— dew skee noh-teek

— wind surfing?
— de la planche à voile?
— der lah plansh ah vwahl

Sport and recreation

Can we play — tennis?
Peut-on jouer — au tennis?
per-ton joo-ay — oh tay-nees

— golf?
— au golf?
— oh gohlf

Can we play — volleyball?
Peut-on jouer — au volley-ball?
per-ton joo-ay — oh voh-lay-bohl

Can I rent the equipment?
Puis-je louer le matériel?
pweej loo-ay ler mah-tay-ryail

Can we go riding?
Peut-on monter à cheval?
per-ton mon-tay ah sher-vahl

Where can we fish?
Où peut-on faire de la pêche?
oo per-ton fair der lah paish

Do I need a permit?
Ai-je besoin d'un permis?
ai-jer ber-zwern dern pair-mee

Is there a heated swimming pool?
Y a-t-il une piscine chauffée?
ee-ah-teel ewn pee-seen shoh-fay

Entertainment

Is there — a disco?
Y a-t-il — une disco(thèque)?
ee-ah-teel — ewn dees-koh(taik)

Entertainment

Is there — a good nightclub?
Y a-t-il — une bonne boîte de nuit?
ee-ah-teel — ewn bohn bwaht der nwee

— a theatre?
— un théâtre?
— ern tay-ahtr

— a casino?
— un casino
— ern kah-see-noh

Are there any films in English?
Y a-t-il des films en anglais?
ee-ah-teel day feelm zan an-glay

How much is it per person?
Ça coûte combien par personne?
Sah koot kohm-byern pahr pair-sohn

Two stall tickets, please
Deux orchestres, s'il vous plaît
der-zohr-kaistr, seel voo play

Two tickets, please
Deux billets, s'il vous plaît
der bee-yay, seel voo play

How much is it to get in?
C'est combien pour l'entrée?
sai kohm-byern poor lan-tray

Is there a reduction for children?
Y a-t-il une réduction pour les enfants?
ee-ah-teel ewn ray-dewk-syon poor lay zan-fan

Sightseeing

Are there any — boat trips on the river?
   Y a-t-il — des promenades en bateau sur la rivière?
   ee-ah-teel — day prohm-nahd an bah-toh sewr lah
      reevyair

   — guided tours of the castle?
   — des visites guidées du château?
   — day vee-seet gee-day dew shah-toh

   — guided tours?
   — des visites guidées?
   — day vee-seet gee-day

What is the admission charge?
Combien coûte le billet?
kohm-hyern koot ler bee-yay

What is there to see here?
Qu'y a-t-il à voir par ici?
kyah-teel ah vwahr pahr ee-see

Can we go up to the top?
Peut-on aller jusqu'en haut?
per-ton ah-lay jewsk an oh

Sightseeing

What time does the gallery open?
A quelle heure ouvre la galerie?
ah kail err oovr lah gah-lai-ree

Can I take photos?
Puis-je prendre des photos?
pweej prandr day foh-toh

Can I use flash?
Puis-je utiliser le flash?
pweej ew-tee-lee-zay ler flahsh

When is the bus tour?
A quelle heure est l'excursion en autocar?
ah kail err ai laiks-kewr-syon an oh-toh-kahr

How long does the tour take?
Combien de temps dure l'excursion?
kohm-byern der tan dewr laiks-kewr-syon

What is this building?
Cet édifice, qu'est-ce que c'est?
sait ay-dee-fees, kais ker sai

When was it built?
Quand a-t-il été construit?
kan tah-teel ay-tay kon-strwee

Is it open to the public?
Est-il ouvert au public?
ai-teel oo-vair oh pewb-leek

Can we go in?
Peut-on entrer?
per-ton an-tray

Do you have a guide book?
Avez-vous un guide?
ah-vay voo zern geed

Is there a tour of the cathedral?
Y a-t-il une visite de la cathédrale?
ee-ah-teel ewn vee-seet der lah kah-tay-drahl

Is there an English-speaking guide?
Y a-t-il un guide anglophone?
ee-ah-teel ern geed an-gloh-fohn

Is this the best view?
Est-ce le plus beau panorama?
ais ler plew boh pah-noh-rah-mah

Souvenirs

Where can I buy postcards?
Où puis-je acheter des cartes postales?
oo pweej ahsh-tay day kahrt pohs-tahl

Where can we buy souvenirs?
Où peut-on acheter des souvenirs?
oo per ton ahsh-tay day soo-ver-neer

Going to church

Have you got an English guidebook?
Avez-vous un guide en anglais?
ah-vay voo zern geed an an-glay

Have you got any colour slides?
Avez-vous des diapos(itives) en couleur?
ah-vay voo day dyah-poh(see-teev) an koo-lerr

How much does that cost?
C'est combien, s'il vous plaît?
sai kohm-byern, seel voo play

Have you got anything cheaper?
Avez-vous quelque chose de moins cher?
ah-vay voo kail-ker shohz der mwan shair

Going to church

Where is — the Catholic church?
Où est — l'église catholique?
oo ai — lay-gleez kah-toh-leek

— the Baptist church?
— l'église baptiste?
— lay-gleez bahp-teest

— the mosque?
— la mosquée?
— lah mohs-kay

Where is — the Protestant church?
  Où est — le temple?
   oo ai — ler tanpl

        — the synagogue?
        — la synagogue?
        — *lah seen-ah-gohg*

What time is the service?
A quelle heure est la messe?
ah kail err ai lah mais

I would like to see — a priest
  Je voudrais voir — un prêtre
jer voo-dray vwahr — ern praitr

        — a minister
        — un pasteur
        — *ern pahs-terr*

        — a rabbi
        — un rabbin
        — *ern rah-bern*

SHOPPING

General information

Nowhere is the culture gap between Britain and France clearer than in the matter of shopping. Department stores and small supermarkets have little importance outside Paris and other very big city centres; instead, in every town and in most villages, there are small, specialised shops and boutiques, while on the outskirts of large towns can be found furniture and DIY warehouses and enormous hypermarkets.

It is the care and flair that the French put into the preparation of food that most visitors find remarkable. Stalls and counters provide a feast for the eyes and a delight to the nose. Every town and sizeable village has regular markets, from early morning to midday once or twice a week, which are the best source for fresh fruit and vegetables and often for cheese, meat and fish; prices are always lower than in the shops. The hypermarkets, too, are cheap and offer a huge range of high-quality food plus all sorts of other goods. Among the best bargains are table wine, bottled beer, coffee beans, olive oil and cast-iron cookware.

Most shops open early in the morning and stay open well

General phrases and requests

into the evening but have a long midday break; food shops – particularly bakers, cake shops and delicatessens – are often open on Sunday morning. Many shops close all day on Monday. Hypermarket opening hours are long – usually 8am or 10am to 10pm, including Mondays.

Les médicaments (medicines) are sold in *pharmacies,* cosmetics in *parfumeries.* You can get stamps (*des timbres*) from a general newsagent (*marchand de journaux*), a tobacconist (*bureau de tabac*) or a bookshop (*librairie*).

General phrases and requests

I would like that one
Je voudrais celui-là
jer voo-dray ser-lwee-lah

No, the other one
Non, l'autre
non, lohtr

I would like that one over there?
Je voudrais l'autre, là-bas
jer voo-dray lohtr, lah-bah

I would like the other one
Je voudrais l'autre
jer voo-dray lohtr

General phrases and requests

Can I have a carrier bag?
Avez-vous un sac?
ah-vay voo zern sahk

Can I pay for air insurance?
Puis-je payer l'assurance pour un colis avion?
pweej pay-yay lah-sew-rans poor ern koh-lee ah-vyon

Can I see that umbrella?
Puis-je regarder ce parapluie?
pweej rer-gahr-day ser pah-rah-plwee

Can I use traveller's cheques?
Puis-je utiliser des chèques de voyage?
pweej ew-tee-lee-zay day shaik der voh-yahj

Can you deliver it to my hotel?
Pouvez-vous le livrer à mon hôtel?
poo-vay voo ler leev-ray ah mon oh-tail

Have you got anything cheaper?
Avez-vous quelque chose de moins cher?
ah-vay voo kail-ker shohz der mwan shair

How much does that cost?
C'est combien, s'il vous plaît?
sai kohm-byern, seel voo play

How much is it per kilo?
C'est combien le kilo?
sai kohm-byern ler kee-loh

General phrases and requests

How much is it per metre?
C'est combien le mètre?
sai kohm-byern ler maitr

I am looking for a souvenir
Je cherche un souvenir
jer shairsh ern soov-neer

I do not like it
Cela ne me plaît pas
ser-lah ner mer plai pah

I like this one
Ceci me plaît
ser-see mer plai

I will take this one
Je vais prendre celui-ci
jer vai prandr ser-lwee-see

Is there a reduction for children?
Y a-t-il une réduction pour les enfants?
ee-ah-teel ewn ray-dewk-syon poor lay zan-fan

Please forward a receipt to this address
Envoyez un reçu à cette adresse, je vous prie
an-vwah-yay ern rer-sew ah sait ah-drais, jer voo pree

Please pack it for shipment
Emballez-le pour l'expédition, s'il vous plaît
an-bah-lay-ler poor laiks-pay-dee-syon, seel voo play

General phrases and requests

Please wrap it up for me
Emballez-le, je vous prie
an-bah-lay-ler, jer voo pree

There is no need to wrap it
Ce n'est pas la peine de l'emballer
ser nai pah lah pain der lan-bah-lay

We need to buy some food
Il faut acheter de la nourriture
eel foh ahsh-tay der lah noo-ree-tewr

Where can I buy cassette tapes and compact discs?
Où puis-je trouver des cassettes et des disques laser?
oo pwee-jer troo-vay day kah-sait ay day deesk lah-zair

Where can I buy some clothes?
Où puis-je acheter des vêtements?
oo pweej ahsh-tay day vait-man

Where can I buy tapes for my camcorder?
Où puis-je trouver des cassettes pour mon caméscope?
oo pweej troo-vay day kah-sait poor mon kah-may-skohp

Where can I get my camcorder repaired?
Où puis-je faire réparer mon caméscope?
oo pweej fair ray-pah-ray mon kah-may-skohp

Will you send it by air freight?
Pouvez-vous l'expédier par avion?
poo-vay voo laiks-pay-dyay pahr ah-vyon

Where is the children's department?
Où est le rayon enfants?
oo ai ler rah-yon an-fan

Where is the food department?
Où est le rayon alimentation?
oo ai ler rah-yon ah-lee-man-tah-syon

Specialist food shops

Boulangeries and pâtisseries

Bread and pastry shops Most French bread doesn't keep long, so it has to be very fresh. The traditional loaf is the long, thin, crusty white *baguette,* sold in various sizes; longer-lasting breads – wholemeal, rye and country loaves – are increasingly available. Breakfast treats include *croissants* and the sweet *brioche* and *pain au chocolat,* flaky pastry with chocolate filling.

Patisseries are for serious cakes, freshly made on the premises. Shops generally have a particular speciality – such as rich chocolate *gâteaux*, fruit tarts, fancy biscuits or hand-made chocolates.

Boucheries and charcuteries

Butchers' and delicatessens High quality and meticulous preparation are the trademarks of a French butcher so prices may seem high. The range of produce is usually much larger than at home – including a wider range of poultry, game, rabbits and hares – and cuts of meat may be different. Minced

Specialist food shops

meat (*hâché*) can be prepared in several qualities, including the ultra-lean *tartare* for eating raw.

French delicatessens provide pâtés and terrines, quiches and pizzas, puddings and pies, hams and sausages, and ready-made *hors d'oeuvre* and sometimes main dishes such as beef cooked in wine.

Poissonneries

Fish shops There are far more fish stalls in France than proper fish shops. Even inland, there's a surprisingly good choice, ranging from the tiniest winkle to tunny fish of massive proportions, invariably very fresh. There are plenty of fish that you can take home and simply grill – sole, trout, prawns, fresh sardines, for example – and also many less familiar sights and some that are suitable only for soups and stews. Fishmongers will willingly clean and gut (*vider*) the fish for you.

Oysters are excellent value. By combining oysters with mussels, prawns, clams and other seafood you can make up your own *plateau de fruits de mer* – an expensive dish in any restaurant but one that you can put together fairly cheaply near the coast.

Crémeries, fromageries and épiceries

Dairy, cheese and grocers' shops In regions rich in dairy products, specialist *crémeries* (dairies) are common. Milk is commonly UHT – heat-treated and long-lasting, which bears no resemblance to real milk; non-UHT pasteurised milk is sometimes hard to find.

Buying groceries

The widest variety of cheese comes from a *fromagerie*. Made from cows', goats' or ewes' milk, it ranges from mild to very strong and smelly; it's worth trying Brie or Camembert made from unpasteurised milk (*lait cru*), which is quite unlike the average supermarket product at home.

Grocers' shops (*épiceries*) are useful, particularly for high-quality tins or jars of vegetables or soups.

Buying groceries

I would like — a kilo of potatoes
Je voudrais — un kilo de pommes de terre
jer voo-dray — ern kee-loh der pohm der tair

       — a bar of chocolate
       — une tablette de chocolat
       — ewn tah-blait der shoh-koh-lah

       — a litre of milk
       — un litre de lait
       — ern leetr der lay

       — two steaks
       — deux biftecks
       — der beef-taik

Can I have — some sugar, please?
Je voudrais — du sucre, s'il vous plaît
jer voo-dray— dew sewkr, seel voo play

Groceries

Can I have — a bottle of wine, please?
Je voudrais — une bouteille de vin, s'il vous plaît
jer voo-dray— ewn boo-tery der vern, seel voo play

— **5 slices of ham, please?**
— cinq tranches de jambon, s'il vous plaît
— *sank transh der jan-bon, seel voo play*

— **100 g of ground coffee?**
— cent grammes de café moulu, s'il vous plaît
— *san grahm der kah-fay moo-lew, seel voo play*

— **half a dozen eggs, please?**
— six oeufs, s'il vous plaît
— *see zer, seel voo play*

— **half a kilo of butter, please?**
— une livre de beurre, s'il vous plaît
— *ewn leevr der berr, seel voo play*

Groceries

groceries
provisions
proh-vee-syon

baby food
aliments pour bébés
ah-lee-man poor bay-bay

biscuits
biscuits
bees-kwee

bread
pain
pern

174

butter
beurre
berr

cheese
fromage
froh-mahj

coffee
café
kah-fay

cream
crème
kraim

eggs
oeufs
er

flour
farine
fah-reen

jam
confiture
kon-fee-tewr

margarine
margarine
mahr-gah-reen

milk
lait
lay

mustard
moutarde
moo-tahrd

oil
huile
weel

pepper
poivre
pwahvr

rice
riz
ree

salt
sel
sail

soup
soupe
soop

sugar
sucre
sewkr

Meat and fish

tea	**yoghurt**
thé	yaourt
tay	*yah-oor*

Meat and fish

meat	**kidneys**
viande	rognons
vee-and	*rohn-yon*
beef	**pork**
boeuf	porc
berf	*pohr*
chicken	**veal**
poulet	veau
poo-lay	*voh*
ham	**fish**
jambon	poisson
jan-bon	*pwah-son*
lamb	**cod**
agneau	morue
ahn-yoh	*moh-rew*
liver	**herring**
foie	hareng
fwah	*ah-raing*

mussels	**sole**
moules	sole
mool	*sohl*

At the newsagent's

I would like — some postage stamps
Je voudrais — des timbres
jer voo-dray — day termbr

— **postcards**
— des cartes postales
— *day kahrt pohs-tahl*

I need — some adhesive tape
Il me faut — du scotch
eel mer foh — dew skohtsh

— **a bottle of ink**
— une bouteille d'encre
— *zewn boo-tery dankr*

— **a pen**
— un stylo
— *zern stee-loh*

— **a pencil**
— un crayon
— *zern kray-yon*

177

At the newsagent's

I need — some envelopes
Il me faut — des enveloppes
eel me foh — day zan-vai-lohp

— some note paper
— du papier à lettres
— dew pah-pyay ah laitr

Do you have — English paperbacks?
Avez-vous — des livres de poche anglais?
ah-vay voo — day leevr der pohsh an-glay

— a local map?
— une carte de la région?
— ewn kahrt der lah ray-jyon

— street maps?
— des plans de ville?
— day plan der veel

— a road map?
— une carte routière?
— zewn kahrt roo-tyair

— coloured pencils?
— des crayons de couleur?
— day kray-yon der koo-lerr

— felt pens?
— des stylos-feutres?
— day stee-loh fertr

Do you have — drawing paper?
  Avez-vous — du papier à dessin?
  ah-vay voo — dew pah-pyay ah dai-sern

       — English newspapers?
       — des journaux anglais?
       — day joor-noh zan-glay

       — English books?
       — des livres anglais?
       — day leevr zan-glay

At the tobacconist's

Do you have— cigarette papers?
  Avez-vous — du papier à cigarettes?
  ah-vay voo — dew pah-pyay ah see-gah-rait

       — a box of matches?
       — une boîte d'allumettes?
       — ewn bwaht dah-lew-mait

       — a cigar?
       — un cigare?
       — ern see-gahr

       — a cigarette lighter?
       — un briquet?
       — ern bree-kay

At the tobacconist's

Do you have— a pipe?
  Avez-vous — une pipe?
ah-vay vous — ewn peep

       — a gas (butane) refill?
       — une cartouche de gaz?
       — ewn kahr-toosh der gahz

       — a pouch of pipe tobacco?
       — un paquet de tabac à pipe?
       — ern pah-kay der tah-bahk ah peep

       — some pipe cleaners?
       — des cure-pipes?
       — day kewr-peep

A packet of...please
Un paquet de... s'il vous plaît
ern pah-kay der... seel voo play

A packet of...please, with filter tips
Un paquet de... s'il vous plaît, à bout filtre
ern pah-kay der... seel voo play, ah boo feeltr

A packet of...please, without filters
Un paquet de... s'il vous plaît, sans filtre
ern pah-kay der... seel voo play, san feeltr

Have you got any — English brands?
      Avez-vous — des cigarettes anglaises?
      ah-vay voo — day see-gah-rait an-glaiz

Have you got any — American brands?
Avez vous — des cigarettes américaines?
ah-vay vous — day see-gah-rait ah-may-ree-kain

— rolling tobacco?
— du tabac à cigarettes?
— dew tah-bahk ah see-gaa-rait

At the chemist's

I need some high-protection suntan cream
Je veux une crème solaire pour peau délicate
jer ver ewn kraim soh-lair poor poh day-lee-kaht

Do you sell sunglasses?
Vendez-vous des lunettes de soleil?
van-day voo day lew-nait der soh-lery

Can you give me something for — insect bites?
Avez-vous quelque chose contre — les piqûres d'insectes?
ah-vay voo kail-ker shohz kawntr — lay pee-kewr dern-saikt

— an upset stomach?
— le mal à l'estomac?
— ler mahl ah lais-toh-mah

— a cold?
— un rhume?
— ern rewm

At the chemist's

Can you give me something for — a cough?
Avez-vous quelque-chose contre— une toux?
ah-vay voo kail-ker shohz kawntr — ewn too

> **— a headache?**
> — les maux de tête?
> — *lay moh der tait*

> **— a sore throat?**
> —un mal de gorge?
> — *ern mahl der gohrj*

> **— hay fever?**
> — le rhume des foins?
> — *ler rewm day fwern*

> **— toothache?**
> — le mal aux dents?
> — *ler mahl oh dan*

> **— sunburn?**
> — un coup de soleil?
> — *ern koo der soh-lery*

Do I need a prescription?
Ai-je besoin d'une ordonnance?
ay-jer ber-zwern dewn ohr-doh-nans

How many do I take?
Combien de cachets dois-je prendre?
kohm-byern der kah-shay dwah-jer prandr

How often do I take them?
Je les prends tous les combien?
jer lay pran too lay kohm-byern

Are they safe for children to take?
Est-ce qu'ils conviennent aux enfants?
ais keel kon-vyain oh zan-fan

Medicines and toiletries

aftershave
aftershave
ahf-tair-shayv

antihistamine
antihistamine
an-tees-tah-meen

antiseptic
antiseptique
an-tee-saip-teek

aspirin
aspirine
ahs-pee-reen

band-aid
pansement adhésif
pans-man ahd-ay-zeef

bandage
pansement
pans-man

bath salt
sels de bain
sail der bern

bubble bath
bain mousseux
bern moo-ser

cleansing milk
lait démaquillant
lay day-mah-kee-yan

contraceptive
préservatif
pray-sair-vah-teef

Medicines and toiletries

cotton wool
coton hydrophile
koh-ton eed-roh-feel

deodorant
déodorant
day-oh-doh-ran

disinfectant
désinfectant
day-zern-faik-tan

eau de Cologne
eau de Cologne
oh der koh-lohn

eye shadow
fard à paupières
fahr dah poh-pyair

hair spray
laque
lahk

hand cream
crème pour les mains
kraim poor lay mern

insect repellent
insectifuge
an-saik-tee-fewj

kleenex
kleenex
klee-naiks

laxative
laxatif
lahk-sah-teef

lipstick
rouge à lèvres
rooj ah laivr

mascara
mascara
mahs-kah-rah

mouthwash
bain de bouche
bern der boosh

nail file
lime à ongles
leem ah ongl

nail varnish remover
dissolvant
dee-sohl-van

nail varnish
vernis à ongles
vair-nee ah ongl

perfume
parfum
pahr-fern

powder
poudre
poodr

razor blades
lames de rasoir
lahm der rah-zwahr

sanitary towels
serviettes hygiéniques
sair-vyait ee-jay-neek

shampoo
shampooing
shahm-poo-eeng

shaving cream
crème à raser
kraim ah rah-zay

skin moisturiser
crème hydratante
kraim eed-rah-tant

soap
savon
sah-von

suntan oil
crème solaire
kraim soh-lair

talc
talc
tahlk

toilet water
eau de toilette
oh der twah-lait

toothpaste
dentifrice
dan-tee-frees

Shopping for clothes

I am just looking, thank you
Je ne fais que regarder, merci
jer ner fai ker rer-gahr-day, mair-see

Shopping for clothes

I like that one there
J'aime bien celui-là
jaim byern ser-lwee-lah

I like the one in the window
J'aime bien celui qui est en vitrine
jaim byern ser-lwee kee ai an vee-treen

I like this one
J'aime bien celui-ci
jaim byern ser-lwee-see

I like it
Il me plaît
eel mer plai

I do not like it
Il ne me plaît pas
eel ner mer plai pah

I will take it
Je le prends
jer ler pran

Can I change it if it does not fit?
Puis-je le rapporter s'il ne me va pas?
pweej ler rah-pohr-tay seel ner mer vah pah

Can you please measure me?
Pouvez-vous prendre mes mesures, s'il vous plaît?
poo-vay voo prandr may mer-sewr, seel voo play

Shopping for clothes

Have you got a larger size?
Avez-vous une taille plus grande?
ah-vay voo ewn tah-ee plew grand

Have you got this in other colours?
Avez-vous ceci dans une autre teinte?
ah-vay voo ser-see dan zewn ohtr ternt

I take a large shoe size
Je chausse grand
jer shohs gran

I take continental size ... 43
Je chausse du ... 43
jer shohs dew ... kah-rant trwah

I would like this suit
Je voudrais ce costume
jer voo-dray ser koh-stewm

I would like one with a zip
J'en voudrais un avec une fermeture éclair
jan voo-dray ern ah-vaik ewn fairm-tewr ay-klair

I would like this hat
Je voudrais ce chapeau
jer voo-dray ser shah-poh

I would like a smaller size
Je voudrais une taille plus petite
jer voo-dray ewn tah-ee plew per-teet

Shopping for clothes

Where are the changing (dressing) rooms?
Où sont les cabines d'essayage?
oo son lay kah-been dai-say-yahj

Where can I try it on?
Où puis-je l'essayer?
oo pweej lai-say-yay

Is it too long?
Est-ce trop long?
ais troh lon

Is it too short?
Est-ce trop court?
ais troh koor

Is there a full-length mirror?
Y a-t-il un grand miroir?
ee-ah-teel ern gran meer-wahr

Is this all you have?
Est-ce tout ce que vous avez?
ais toos ker voo zah-vay

It does not fit
Ce n'est pas à ma taille
Ser nai pahz ah mah tahy

It does not suit me
Il ne me va pas
eel ner mer vah pah

188

Clothes and accessories

May I see it in daylight?
Puis-je le regarder à la lumière du jour?
pwee-jer ler rer-gahr-day ah lah lew-myair dew joor

Is it drip-dry?
Faut-il le repasser?
foh-teel ler rer-pah-say

Is it dry-clean only?
Faut-il le nettoyer à sec seulement?
foh-teel ler nai-twah-yay ah saik serl-man

Is it machine washable?
Est-ce lavable à la machine?
ais lah-vahbl ah lah mah-sheen

What is it made of?
C'est en quel tissu?
sai tan kail tee-sew

Will it shrink?
Est-ce que ça rétrécit?
ais ker sah ray-tray-see

Clothes and accessories

acrylic
acrylique
ah-kree-leek

bracelet
bracelet
brahs-lay

Clothes and accessories

belt
ceinture
sern-tewr

blouse
chemisier
sher-mee-zyay

bra
soutien-gorge
soo-tyern gohrj

brooch
broche
brohsh

button
bouton
boo-ton

cardigan
gilet
jee-lay

coat
manteau
man-toh

corduroy
velours côtelé
ver-loor koht-lay

denim
jean
djeen

dress
robe
rohb

dungarees
salopette
sah-loh-pait

earrings
boucles d'oreille
bookl doh-ray

fur
fourrure
foo-rewr

gloves
gants
gan

handbag
sac à main
sahk ah mern

handkerchief
mouchoir
moo-shwahr

Clothes and accessories

hat
chapeau
shah-poh

jacket
veste
vaist

jeans
jean
djeen

jersey
tricot
tree-koh

lace
dentelle
dan-tail

leather
cuir
kweer

linen
(toile de) lin
twahl der lern

necklace
collier
koh-lyay

night-dress
chemise de nuit
sher-meez der nwee

nylon
nylon
nee-lon

panties
slip
sleep

pendant
pendentif
pan-dan-teef

polyester
polyester
pohl-yais-tair

pullover
pull(-over)
pewl(-oh-vair)

purse
porte-monnaie
pohrt moh-nai

pyjamas
pyjama
pee-jah-mah

191

Clothes and accessories

raincoat
imper(méable)
ern-pair(-may-ahbl)

rayon
rayonne
ray-ohn

ring
bague
bahg

sandals
sandales
san-dahl

scarf
écharpe
ay-shahrp

shirt
chemise
sher-meez

shorts
short
shohrt

silk
soie
swah

skirt
jupe
jewp

slip
combinaison
kohm-bee-nay-son

socks
chaussettes
shoh-sait

stockings
bas
bah

suede
daim
derm

suit (men's)
complet, costume
kohm-plai, kostoom

suit (women's)
tailleur
tah-yerr

sweater
chandail
shan-dah-ee

Clothes and accessories

swimming trunks
maillot de bain
mah-yoh der bern

swimsuit
costume de bain
kohs-tewm der bern

t-shirt
T-shirt
tee-shairt

tie
cravate
krah-vaht

tights
collant
koh-lan

towel
serviette
sair-vyait

trousers
pantalon
pan-tah-lon

umbrella
parapluie
pah-rah-plwee

underpants
slip
sleep

underskirt
jupon
jew-pon

velvet
velours
ver-loor

vest
maillot de corps
mah-yoh der kohr

watch
montre
montr

wool
laine
lain

zip
fermeture éclair
fairm-tewr ay-klair

Photography

Can you develop this film, please?
Pouvez-vous développer cette pellicule, s'il vous plaît?
poo-vay voo dayv-loh-pay sait pay-lee-kewl, seel voo play

I would like this photo enlarged
Je voudrais un agrandissement de cette photo
jer voo-dray zern ah-gran-dees-man der sait foh-toh

I would like two prints of this one
Je voudrais deux copies de cette photo
jer voo-dray der koh-pee der sait foh-toh

When will the photos be ready?
Quand est-ce que les photos seront prêtes?
kan ais ker lay foh-toh ser-ron prait

I need a film for — this camera
Je voudrais une pellicule pour — cet appareil
jer voo-dray zewn pay-lee-kewl poor — sait ah-pah-rery

— this camcorder
— ce caméscope
— ser kah-may-skohp

— this cine camera
— cette caméra
— sait kah-may-rah

194

I need a film for — this video camera
Je voudrais une pellicule pour — cette caméra vidéo
jer voo-dray zewn pay-lee-kewl poor — sait kah-may-rah
vee-dyoh

I want a black and white film
Je veux une pellicule noir et blanc
jer ver ewn pay-lee-kewl nwahr ay blan

I want batteries for the flash
Je veux des piles pour le flash
jer ver day peel poor ler flahsh

I want a colour slide film
Je veux une pellicule couleur pour diapos(itives)
jer ver zewn pay-lee-kewl koo-lerr poor dyah-poh(-see-teev)

I want a colour print film
Je veux une pellicule couleur
jer ver zewn pay-lee-kewl koo-lerr

Camera repairs

I am having trouble with my camera
J'ai des problèmes avec mon appareil
jay day proh-blaim ah-vaik moh nah-pah-rery

There is something wrong with my camera
Mon appareil ne marche plus
moh nah-pah-rery ner mahrsh plew

Camera parts

This is broken
C'est cassé
sai kah-say

Where can I get my camera repaired?
Où puis-je faire réparer mon appareil?
oo pweej fair ray-pah-ray moh nah-pah-rery

Have you got a spare part for this?
Avez-vous une pièce de rechange pour ceci?
ah-vay voo zewn pyais der rer-shanj poor ser-see

The film is jammed
La pellicule est coincée
lah pay-lee-kewl ai kwern-say

Camera parts

accessory
accessoire
ahk-sai-swahr

blue filter
filtre bleu
feeltr bler

cassette
cassette
kah-sait

cartridge
cartouche
kahr-toosh

camcorder
caméscope
kah-may-skohp

cine camera
caméra
kah-may-rah

distance
distance
dees-tans

enlargement
agrandissement
ah-gran-dees-man

exposure
pose
pohz

exposure meter
posemètre
pohz-maitr

flash
flash
flahsh

flash bulb
ampoule de flash
an-pool der flahsh

flash cube
cube de flash
kewb der flahsh

focal distance
distance focale
dees-tans foh-kahl

focus
mise au point
meez oh pwan

in focus
net
nay

out of focus
flou
floo

image
image
ee-mahj

lens
objectif
ohb-jaik-teef

lens cover
bouchon d'objectif
boo-shon dohb-jaik-teef

over exposed
surexposé
sewr-aiks-poh-zay

picture
photo
foh-toh

Camera parts

projector
projecteur
proh-jaik-terr

print
épreuve
ay-prerv

negative
négatif
nay-gah-teef

red filter
filtre rouge
feeltr rooj

reel
bobine
boh-been

shade
nuance
new-ans

slide
diapositive
dyah-poh-zee-teef

shutter
obturateur
ohb-tew-rah-terr

shutter speed
vitesse d'obturateur
vee-tais dohb-tew-rah-terr

transparency
transparent
trans-pah-ran

tripod
tripode
tree-pohd

under exposed
sous-exposé
soo-zaiks-poh-zay

viewfinder
viseur
vee-zerr

wide-angle lens
objectif grand angle
ohb-jaik-teef gran tangl

At the hairdresser's

I would like to make an appointment
Je voudrais prendre rendez-vous
jer voo-dray prandr ran-day-voo

I want a haircut
Je veux me faire couper les cheveux
jer ver mer fair koo-pay lay sher-ver

Please cut my hair short
Coupez mes cheveux court, s'il vous plaît
koo-pay may sher-ver koor, seel voo play

Please cut my hair in a fringe
Coupez mes cheveux avec une frange
koo-pay may sher-ver ah-vaik ewn franjr

Take a little more off the back
Dégagez un peu plus à l'arrière
day-gah-jay ern per plews ah lah-ryair

I would like — a trim
  Je voudrais — une coupe d'entretien
jer voo-dray — ewn koop dantr-tyern

> **— a conditioner**
>   — du baume démêlant
>   *— dew bohm day-mai-lan*

199

At the hairdresser's

I would like — a perm
Je voudrais — une permanente
jer voo-dray — ewn pair-mah-nant

— my hair streaked
— des mèches
— day maish

— a blow-dry
— un brushing
— ern broo-sheeng

— hair spray
— de la laque
— der lah lahk

— my hair dyed
— me les faire teindre
— mer lay fair terndr

— a shampoo and cut
— un shampooing et une coupe
— ern shahm-pweeng ay ewn koop

— a shampoo and set
— un shampooing et une mise en plis
— ern shahm pweeng ay ewn mee zan plee

That is fine, thank you
C'est parfait, merci
sai pahr-fai, mair-see

Not too much off
Pas trop
pah troh

The dryer is too hot
Le séchoir est trop chaud
ler say-shwahr ai troh shoh

The water is too hot
L'eau est trop chaude
loh ai troh shohd

Laundry

Is there a launderette nearby?
Y a-t-il une laverie automatique près d'ici?
ee-ah-teel ewn lahv-ree oh-toh-mah-teek prai dee-see

Can you clean this skirt?
Pouvez-vous laver cette jupe?
poo-vay voo lah-vay sait jewp

Can you clean and press these shirts?
Pouvez-vous laver et repasser ces chemises?
poo-vay voo lah-vay ay rer-pah-say say sher-meez

Can you wash these clothes?
Pouvez-vous laver ces vêtements?
poo-vay voo lah-vay say vait-man

Laundry

This stain is — oil
Cette tache est — de l'huile
sait tahsh ai — der lweel

        — blood
        — du sang
        — dew san

        — coffee
        — du café
        — dew kah-fay

        — ink
        — de l'encre
        — der lankr

This fabric is — delicate
Ce tissu est — fin
ser tee-sew ai — fern

        — damaged
        — endommagé
        — tan-doh-mah-jay

        — torn
        — déchiré
        — day-shee-ray

Can you do it quickly?
Pouvez-vous le faire rapidement?
poo-vay voo ler fair rah-peed-man

When should I come back?
Quand dois-je revenir?
kan dwah-jer rerv-neer

When will my clothes be ready?
Quand puis-je passer prendre mes vêtements?
kan pwee-jer pah-say prandr may vait-man

How does the machine work?
Comment marche cette machine?
koh-man mahrsh sait mah-sheen

How long will it take?
Il y en a pour combien de temps?
eel yan ah poor kohm-byern der tan

I have lost my dry cleaning ticket
J'ai perdu mon coupon de nettoyage à sec
jay pair-dew mon koo-pon der nai-twah-yahj ah saik

General repairs

Can you repair it?
Pouvez-vous le réparer?
poo-vay voo ler ray-pah-ray

Can you repair them?
Pouvez-vous les réparer?
poo-vay voo lay ray-pah-ray

General repairs

Would you have a look at this please?
Pourriez-vous y jeter un coup d'oeil, s'il vous plaît?
poo-ryay voo zee jer-tay an koo dery, seel voo play

Here is the guarantee
Voici la garantie
vwah-see lah gah-ran-tee

I need new heels on these shoes
Ces chaussures ont besoin de talons neufs
say shoh-sewr on ber-zwern der tah-lon nerf

I need them in a hurry
J'en ai besoin aussitôt que possible
john ay ber-zwern oh-see-toh ker poh-seebl

I will come back later
Je reviens plus tard
jer rer-vyern plew tahr

I will come back in an hour
Je reviens dans une heure
jer rer-vyern dan zewn err

Please send it to this address
Expédiez-le à cette adresse, s'il vous plaît
aiks-pay-dyay ler ah sait ah-drais, seel voo play

At the post office

Postage stamps are available at post offices (*bureaux de post* or *PTT* – pronounced *pay tay tay*) and from tobacconists (*tabacs*). Post boxes are painted yellow and are usually sited near *tabacs*.

Can I have a telegram form, please?
Donnez-moi un formulaire de télégramme, s'il vous plaît
doh-nay mwah ern fohr-mew-lair der tay-lay-grahm, seel voo play?

Can I have six stamps for postcards to Britain?
Donnez-moi six timbres pour cartes postales pour la Grande-Bretagne
doh-nay mwah see termbr poor kahrt pohs-tahl poor lah grand-brer-tahn

How much is a letter to — Britain?
C'est combien pour une lettre pour — la Grande-Bretagne?
say kohm-byern poor ewn laitr poor— la grand-brer-tahn

— America?
— les États-Unis?
— *lays-ayta-zewni*

12 stamps, please
Douze timbres, s'il vous plaît
dooz termbr, seel voo play

Using the telephone

I need to send this by courier
Je voudrais envoyer ceci par coursier
jer voo-dray an-vwah-yay ser-see pahr koor-syay

I want to send a telegram
Je veux envoyer un télégramme
jer ver an-vwah-yay ern tay-lay-grahm

I want to send this by registered mail
Je veux envoyer ceci en recommandé
jer ver an-vwah-yay ser-see an rer-koh-man-day

I want to send this parcel
Je vex expédier ce colis
jer ver aiks-pay-dyay ser koh-lee

When will it arrive?
Quand arrivera-t-il à destination?
kan tah-reev-rah teel ah days-tee-nah-syon

Can I use my credit card?
Puis-je utiliser ma carte de crédit?
pweej ew-tee-lee-say mah kahrt der kray-dee

Using the telephone

When phoning from France to Britain you must dial 00, then
44, then the area code minus the initial 0, then the subscriber
number. Coin boxes are being phased out so it is essential to

buy a phone card (50- or 120-unit) although many call boxes also accept credit cards. Phone cards can be bought in *tabacs*, newsagents and post offices. If using a coin box, put the money in before dialling the number: they take 50-centimes, 1-franc, 5-franc or 10-franc pieces. For longer calls you may find it more convenient to phone from a major post office. You will be allocated a numbered kiosk with an ordinary phone and receive a bill at the end of the call. The drawback with this method is that you cannot keep track of what you are spending.

Can I use the telephone, please?
Puis-je me servir du téléphone, s'il vous plaît?
pweej mer sair-veer dew tay-lay-fohn, seel voo play

I must make a phone call to Britain
Il me faut téléphoner en Grande-Bretagne
eel mer foh tay-lay-foh-nay an grand-brer-tahn

I want to make a phone call
Je veux téléphoner
jer ver tay-lay-foh-nay

How much is it to phone to Paris?
C'est combien pour téléphoner à Paris?
sai kohm-byern poor tay-lay-foh-nay ah pah-ree

I would like to make a reversed charge (collect) call
Je voudrais téléphoner en PCV
jer voo-dray tay-lay-foh-nay an pay-say-vay

What you may hear

The number I need is...
Le numéro est le...
ler new-may-roh ai ler...

   What is the code for — Britain?
   Quel est l'indicatif pour — la Grande-Bretagne?
kail ai lern-dee-kah-teef poor— lah grand-brer-tahn

      — America?
      — les États-Unis?
      — lays-ayta-zewni

Please, call me back
Rappelez-moi, s'il vous plaît
rah-play mwah, seel voo play

I am sorry. We were cut off
Je suis désolé. On nous a coupés
jer swee day-soh-lay. on noo zah koo-pay

What you may hear

J'essaie d'obtenir votre communication
jai-say dohb-ter-neer vohtr koh-mew-nee-kah-syon
I am trying to connect you

Je ne peux pas obtenir ce numéro
jer ner per pah zohb-ter-neer ser new-may-roh
I cannot get through to this number

Je vous passe Monsieur Brown
jer voo pahs mer-syer Broon
I am putting you through to Mr Brown

La ligne est occupée
lah leen ai toh-kew-pay
The line is engaged (busy)

Le numéro est en dérangement
ler new-may-roh ai an day-ranj-man
The number is out of order

Allez-y, vous êtes en ligne
ah-lay-zee, voo zait an leen
Please go ahead

Changing money

Can I change these traveller's cheques?
Puis-je changer ces chèques de voyage?
pweej shan-jay say shaik der voh-yahj

Can I change these notes (bills)?
Puis-je changer ces billets?
pweej shan-jay say bee-yay

Can I contact my bank to arrange for a transfer?
Puis-je contacter ma banque pour organiser un virement?
pweej kon-tahk-tay mah bank poor ohr-gah-nee-zay ern
*   veer-man*

Changing money

Has my cash arrived?
Est-ce que mes fonds sont arrivés?
ais-ker may fon son tah-ree-vay?

Here is my passport
Voici mon passeport
vwah-see mon pahs-pohr

I would like to cash a cheque with my Eurocheque card
Je voudrais encaisser un chèque avec ma carte Eurochèque
jer voo-dray an-kai-say ern shaik ah-vaik mah kahrt er-roh-shaik

I would like to obtain a cash advance with my credit card
Je voudrais une avance en liquide sur ma carte de crédit
jer voo-dray ewn ah-vans an lee-keed sewr mah kahrt der kray-dee

This is the name and address of my bank
Voici le nom et l'adresse de ma banque
vwah-see ler nohm ay lah-drais der mah bank

What is the rate for sterling?
Quel est le taux de change pour la livre sterling?
kail ai ler toh der shanj poorlah leevr stair-leeng

What is the rate of exchange?
Quel est le taux de change?
kail ai ler toh der shanj

What is your commission?
Quelle est votre commission?
kail ai vohtr koh-mee-syon

HEALTH

Health services

British travellers will need an E111 form, available in post offices, to be entitled to the same health services as French citizens. In France, every stage of treatment incurs a charge but employed French people are entitled to a refund of 70–75 per cent of medical and dental expenses. To qualify for this reimbursement of some of your expenses, find a doctor who is a *médecin conventionné* (the address of a doctor can be found at any *pharmacie*) whom you must ask for the relevant forms, but be prepared for a bit of paperwork when you return home. Prescriptions must be paid for at the *pharmacie*. All travellers, even those from the EU, would be wise to take out travel insurance and medical cover. The number to ring for a medical emergency is 15. The fire brigade are also able to deal with medical emergencies (telephone 18).

What's wrong?

Can I see a doctor?
Puis-je voir un médecin?
pwee-jer vwahr an mayd-sern

What's wrong?

I need a doctor
Je veux voir un médecin
jer ver vwahr an mayd-sern

He has been badly injured
Il a été grièvement blessé
eel ah ay-tay gree-aiv-man blay-say

He has burnt himself
Il s'est brûlé
eel sai brew-lay

He has dislocated his shoulder
Il s'est démis l'épaule
eel sai day-mee lay-pohl

He is hurt
Il s'est fait mal
eel sai fai mahl

He is unconscious
Il a perdu connaissance
eel ah pair-dew koh-nai-sans

She has a temperature
Elle a de la fièvre
ail ah der lah fyaivr

She has been bitten
Elle a été mordue
ail ah ay-tay mohr-dew

What's wrong?

She has sprained her ankle
Elle s'est tordu la cheville
ail sai tohr-dew lah sher-vee

My son has cut himself
Mon fils s'est coupé
mon fees sai koo-pay

My arm is broken
Mon bras est cassé
mon brah ai kah-say

I am badly sunburnt
J'ai attrapé un mauvais coup de soleil
jay ah-trah-pay ern moh-vai koo der soh-lery

I am ill
Je suis malade
jer swee mah-lahd

I am constipated
Je suis constipé
jer swee kon-stee-pay

I am a diabetic
Je suis diabétique
jer swee dyah-bay-teek

I am allergic to penicillin
Je suis allergique à la pénicilline
jer swee zah-lair-jeek ah lah pay-nee-see-leen

What's wrong?

I have — a headache
  J'ai — mal à la tête
  jay — mahl ah lah tait

> **— a pain here**
> — mal là
> *— mahl lah*

> **— a rash here**
> — une éruption là
> *— ewn ay-rewp-syon lah*

> **— sunstroke**
> — une insolation
> *— ewn ern-soh-lah-syon*

> **— been stung**
> — été piqué
> *— ay-tay pee-kay*

> **— a sore throat**
> — mal à la gorge
> *— mahl ah lah gohrj*

> **— an earache**
> — mal aux oreilles
> *— oh zoh-rery*

> **— cramp**
> — une crampe
> *— ewn krahmp*

214

I have — diarrhoea
  J'ai — la diarrhée
  jay — lah dyah-ray

I have been sick
J'ai vomi
jay voh-mee

I have — hurt my arm
Je me suis — fait mal au bras
jer mer swee — fai mahl oh brah

— hurt my leg
  — fait mal à la jambe
  — fai mahl ah lah janb

— pulled a muscle
  — claqué un muscle
  — klah-kay ern mewskl

— cut myself
  — coupé
  — koo-pay

It is — inflamed here
C'est — enflammé là
  say — tan-flah-may lah

— painful to walk
  — douloureux de marcher
  — doo-loo-rer der mahr-shay

215

What's wrong?

It is — painful to breathe
C'est — douloureux de respirer
say — doo-loo-rer der rers-pee-ray

— painful to swallow
— douloureux d'avaler
— doo-loo-rers dah-vah-lay

I feel dizzy
J'ai des étourdissements
jay day zay-toor-dees-man

I feel faint
Je me sens faible
jer mer san faibl

I feel nauseous
J'ai la nausée
jay lah noh-say

I fell
Je suis tombé
jer swee tohm-bay

I cannot sleep
Je n'arrive pas à dormir
jer nah-reev pah ah dohr-meer

I think I have food poisoning
Je crois que j'ai une intoxication alimentaire
jer krwah ker jay ewn ern-tohk-see-kah-syon ah-lee-man-tair

My stomach is upset
J'ai mal à l'estomac
jay mahl ah lais-toh-mah

My tongue is coated
J'ai la langue chargée
jay lah lan-g shahr-jay

There is a swelling here
C'est enflé là
sai tan-flay lah

I need some antibiotics
J'ai besoin d'antibiotiques
jay ber-zwan dan-tee-byoh-teek

I suffer from high blood pressure
Je fais de l'hypertension
jer fai der lee-pair-tan-syon

I am taking these drugs
Je prends ces médicaments
jer pran say may-dee-kah-man

Can you give me a prescription for them?
Pouvez-vous me donner une ordonnance pour ces médicaments?
*poo-vay voo mer doh-nay ewn ohr-doh-nans poor say may-
     dee-kah-man?*

At the hospital

I am on the pill
Je prends la pilule
jer pran lah pee-lewl

I am pregnant
Je suis enceinte
jer swee zan-cernt

My blood group is…
Mon groupe sanguin est…
mon groop san-gwern ai…

I do not know my blood group
Je ne sais pas quel est mon groupe sanguin
jer ner say pah kail ai mon groop san-gwern

At the hospital

Do I have to go into hospital?
Sera-t-il nécessaire de m'hospitaliser?
ser-ra-teel nay-say-sair der mohs-pee-tah-lee-zay

Do I need an operation?
Est-ce qu'il faudra m'opérer?
ais-keel foh-drah moh-pay-ray

Here is my E111 form
Voici mon formulaire E111
vwah-see mon fohr-mew-lair er san-tonz

How do I get reimbursed?
Comment serai-je remboursé?
koh-man ser-raij ran-boor-say

Must I stay in bed?
Dois-je garder le lit?
dwah-jer gahr-day ler lee

When will I be able to travel?
Quand serai-je en état de voyager?
kan ser-raij an ay-tah der voh-yah-jay

Will I be able to go out tomorrow?
Pourrai-je sortir demain?
poo-raij sohr-teer der-mern

Parts of the body

ankle	**bone**
cheville	os
sher-vee	*oh*
arm	**breast**
bras	sein
brah	*sern*
back	**cheek**
dos	joue
doh	*joo*

219

Parts of the body

chest
poitrine
pwah-treen

ear
oreille
oh-rery

elbow
coude
kood

eye
oeil (plural yeux)
ery (yer)

face
visage
vee-sahj

finger
doigt
dwah

foot
pied
pyay

hand
main
mern

heart
coeur
kerr

kidney
rein
rern

knee
genou
jer-noo

leg
jambe
janb

liver
foie
fwah

lungs
poumons
poo-mon

mouth
bouche
boosh

muscle
muscle
mewskl

neck
cou
koo

nose
nez
nay

skin
peau
poh

stomach
estomac, ventre
ais-toh-mah, vahn-tr

throat
gorge
gohrj

wrist
poignet
pwahn-yay

At the dentist's

I have — a toothache
J'ai — mal aux dents
jay — mahl oh dan

— broken a tooth
— une dent cassée
— ewn dan kah-say

I have to see the dentist
Il faut que je voie le dentiste
eel foh ker jer vwah ler dan-teest

My false teeth are broken
Mon dentier est cassé
mon dan-tyay ai kah-say

At the dentist's

My gums are sore
J'ai mal aux gencives
jay mahl oh jan-seev

Can you find out what the trouble is?
Savez-vous ce qui ne va pas?
sah-vay voo ser kee ner vah pah

Please give me an injection
Donnez-moi une piqûre, s'il vous plaît
doh-nay- mwah ewn pee-kewr, seel voo play

That hurts
Ça fait mal
sah fai mahl

The filling has come out
Le plombage a sauté
ler pohm-bahj ah soh-tay

This one hurts
Celle-ci fait mal
sail-see fai mahl

Will you have to take it out?
Faudra-t-il l'arracher?
foh-drah-teel lah-rah-shay

Are you going to fill it?
Allez-vous la plomber?
ah-lay voo lah plohm-bay

FOR YOUR INFORMATION

Numbers

1 un *ern*

2 deux *der*

3 trois *trwah*

4 quatre *kahtr*

5 cinq *sank*

6 six *sees*

7 sept *sait*

8 huit *weet*

9 neuf *nerf*

10 dix *dees*

11 onze *onz*

12 douze *dooz*

13 treize *traiz*

14 quatorze *kah-tohrz*

Numbers

15 quinze *kernz*

16 seize *saiz*

17 dix-sept *deez-sait*

18 dix-huit *deez-weet*

19 dix-neuf *deez-nerf*

20 vingt *vern*

21 vingt et un *vern tay ern*

22 vingt-deux *vernt-der*

23 vingt-trois *vernt-trwah*

24 vingt-quatre *vernt-kahtr*

25 vingt-cinq *vernt-sank*

26 vingt-six *vernt-sees*

27 vingt-sept *vernt-sait*

28 vingt-huit *vernt-weet*

29 vingt-neuf *vernt-nerf*

30 trente *trant*

40 quarante *kah-rant*

50 cinquante *san-kant*

60 soixante *swah-sant*

70 soixante-dix *swah-sant-dees*

80 quatre-vingts *kahtr-vern*

90 quatre-vingt-dix *kahtr-vern-dees*

100 cent *san*

200 deux cents *der san*

300 trois cents *trwah san*

400 quatre cents *kahtr san*

500 cinq cents *sank san*

600 six cents *see san*

700 sept cents *sait san*

800 huit cents *wee san*

900 neuf cents *nerv san*

1000 mille *meel*

2000 deux mille *der meel*

3000 trois mille *trwah meel*

4000 quatre mille *kahtr meel*

1 000 000 un million *an mee-lyon*

Ordinals

1st premier *prer-myay*

2nd deuxième *der-zyaim*

3rd troisième *trwah-zyaim*

4th quatrième *kaht-ryaim*

5th cinquième *sern-kyaim*

n-th énième *ain-yaim*

Fractions and percentages

a half un demi *an der-mee*

a quarter un quart *an kahr*

a third un tiers *an tyair*

two thirds deux tiers *der tyair*

10% dix pour cent *dee poor san*

Days

Sunday dimanche *dee-mansh*

Dates

Monday	lundi	*lern-dee*
Tuesday	mardi	*mahr-dee*
Wednesday	mercredi	*mair-krer-dee*
Thursday	jeudi	*jer-dee*
Friday	vendredi	*van-drer-dee*
Saturday	samedi	*sahm-dee*

Dates

on Friday	vendredi	*van-drer-dee*
next Tuesday	mardi prochain	*mahr-dee proh-shern*
last Tuesday	mardi dernier	*mahr-dee dair-nyay*
yesterday	hier	*ee-air*
today	aujourd'hui	*oh-joor-dwee*
tomorrow	demain	*der-mern*
next week	la semaine prochaine	*lah ser-main proh-shain*
in June	en juin	*an jwern*
July 7th	le sept juillet	*ler sait jwee-yay*
last month	le mois dernier	*ler mwah dair-nyay*

The seasons

spring	printemps *prern-tan*
summer	été *ay-tay*
autumn	automne *oh-tohn*
winter	hiver *ee-vair*

Times of the year

in spring	au printemps *oh prern-tan*
in summer	en été *ohn ay-tay*
in autumn	en automne *ohn oh-tohn*
in winter	en hiver *ohn ee-vair*

Months

January	janvier *jan-vyay*
February	février *fayv-ryay*
March	mars *mahrs*
April	avril *ahv-reel*
May	mai *may*

June	juin *jwern*
July	juillet *jwee-yay*
August	août *oot*
September	septembre *saip-tanbr*
October	octobre *ohk-tohbr*
November	novembre *noh-vanbr*
December	décembre *day-sanbr*

Public holidays

New Year's Day, January 1
Le Jour de l'An
ler joor der lan

Easter Monday
Le lundi de Pâques
le lern-dee der pahk

Labour Day, May 1
La Fête du Travail
lah fait dew trah-vahee

Armistice Day 1945, May 8
Le 8 mai
le weet mai

Public holidays

Ascension Day (40 days after Easter)
La Fête de l'Ascension
lah fait der lah-san-syon

Whit Monday (7th Monday after Easter)
La Fête de la Pentecôte
lah fait der lah pant-koht

Bastille Day, July 14
Le 14 Juillet
ler kah-tohrz jwee-yay

Assumption Day, August 15
La Fête de l'Assomption
la fait der lah-sohmp-syon

All Saints Day, November 1
La Toussaint
lah too-san

Armistice Day 1918, November 11
Le 11 novembre
ler onz noh-vanbr

Christmas Day, December 25
Noël
noh-ail

Colours

black
noir
nwahr

blue
bleu
bler

brown
marron
mah-ron

cream
crème
kraim

fawn
fauve
fohv

gold
doré
doh-ray

green
vert
vair

grey
gris
gree

orange
orange
oh-ranj

pink
rose
rohz

purple
violet
vyoh-lay

red
rouge
rooj

silver
argenté
ahr-jan-tay

tan
ocre
ohkr

Common adjectives

white
blanc
blan

yellow
jaune
john

Common adjectives

bad
mauvais
moh-vay

difficult
difficile
dee-fee-seel

beautiful
beau/magnifique
boh/mah-nee-feek

easy
facile
fah-seel

big
grand
gran

fast
rapide
rah-peed

cheap
bon marché
bon mahr-shay

good
bon/bien
bon/byern

cold
froid
frwah

high
haut
oh

expensive
cher
shair

hot
chaud
shoh

little
petit
per-tee

short
court
koor

long
long
lon

slow
lent
lan

new
nouveau/neuf
noo-voh/nerf

small
petit
per-tee

old
vieux
vee-er

ugly
laid
lay

Signs and notices (see also **Road signs** page 96)

attention
ah-tan-syon
caution

renseignements
ran-sain-man
information

ascenseur
ah-san-serr
lift/elevator

soldes
sohld
sale

sortie
sohr-tee
exit

épuisé
ay-pwee-zay
sold out

Signs and notices

occupé
oh-kew-pay
occupied

libre
leebr
vacant

sonnez
soh-nay
please ring

Objets trouvés
ohb-jay troo-vay
Lost Property Office

poussez
poo-say
push

entrée interdite
an-tray ern-tair-deet
No trespassing

entrée
an-tray
entrance

danger
dan-jay
danger

entrez sans frapper
an-tray san frah-pay
enter without knocking

fermé
fair-may
closed

entrée gratuite
an-tray grah-tweet
no admission charge

poison
pwah-zon
poison

téléphone
tay-lay-fohn
telephone

chaud
shoh
hot

sapeurs-pompiers
sah-perr pohm-pyay
fire brigade

froid
frwah
cold

caisse
kais
cashier

passage interdit
pah-sahj ern-tair-dee
no thoroughfare

entrée interdite
an-tray ern-tair-deet
no entry

hôpital
oh-pee-tahl
hospital

ambulance
an-bew-lans
ambulance

chemin privé
sher-mern pree-vay
private road

piste cyclable
peest seek-lahbl
cycle path

serrez à droite
sai-ray ah drwaht
keep to the right

souvenirs
soov-neer
souvenirs

agence de voyages
ahj-ans der voh-yahj
travel agency

offre spéciale
ohfr spay-syahl
special offer

eau potable
oh poh-tahbl
drinking water

déviation
day-vyah-syon
diversion

tirez
tee-ray
pull

à vendre
ah vandr
for sale

à louer
ah loo-ay
to let/for hire

Signs and notices

tarifs
tah-reef
price list

bienvenue
byern-ver-new
welcome

réservé aux...
ray-sair-vay oh...
allowed only for...

chien méchant
beware of the dog
shee-ern may-shan

police
poh-lees
police

risque d'incendie
reesk dern-san-dee
danger of fire

départs
day-pahr
departures

détritus
day-tree-tews
litter

ouvert
oo-vair
open

sonnez
soh-nay
ring

arrivées
ah-ree-vay
arrivals

école
ay-kohl
school

entrée
an-tray
entrance

horaires
oh-rair
timetable

messieurs
may-syer
gentlemen

dames
dahm
ladies

douane
doo-ahn
customs

bagages
bah-gahj
baggage

banque
bank
bank

police
poh-lees
police

urgence
oor-jans
emergency

réservé
ray-sair-vay
reserved

danger de mort
dan-jay der mohr
danger of death

espace fumeurs
ais-pahs few-merr
smoking area

interdiction de marcher sur le gazon
ern-tair-deek-syon der mahr-shay sewr ler gah-zon
keep off the grass

pour usage externe seulement
poor ew-zahj aiks-tairn serl-man
for external use only

ne pas parler au conducteur en cours de route
ner pah pahr-lay oh kon-dewk-terr an koor der root
It is forbidden to speak to the driver while the bus is moving

ne pas toucher
ner pah too-shay
do not touch

Signs and notices

avertisseur d'incendie
ah-vair-tee-serr dern-san-dee
fire alarm

sortie de secours
sohr-tee der ser-koor
emergency exit

sonnette d'alarme
soh-nait dah-lahrm
communication cord (rail)

interdiction de photographier
ern-tair-deek-syon der foh-toh-grah-fyay
no picture taking

réservé au personnel
ray-sair-vay oh pair-soh-nail
employees only

parking réservé aux résidents
pahr-keeng ray-sair-vay oh ray-zee-dan
parking for residents only

compartiment fumeurs
kohm-pahr-tee-man few-merr
smoking compartment

liquidation des stocks
lee-kee-dah-syon day stohk
closing-down sale

fermé l'après-midi
fair-may lah-prai-mee-dee
closed in the afternoon

ne pas se pencher au dehors
ner pah ser pan-shay oh der-ohr
do not lean out

interdiction de fumer
ern-tair-deek-syon der few-may
no smoking

In an Emergency

Fire brigade   Pompiers *pohm-pyay*   — telephone 18
Ambulance   Ambulance *an-bew-lans* — telephone 15
Police   Police *poh-lees*   — telephone 17

Call –   **an ambulance**
Appelez –   une ambulance
ah-play –   *ewn an-bew-lans*

– the fire brigade
– les pompiers
– *lay pohm-pyay*

– the police
– la police
– *lah poh-lees*

There is a fire
Il y a un incendie
eel-yah ern ern-san-dee

Get a doctor
Appelez un médecin
ah-play ern mayd-sern

My son is lost
Mon fils s'est perdu
mon fees sai pair-dew

My daughter is ill
Ma fille est malade
mah fee ai mah-lahd

Who speaks English?
Qui parle anglais?
kee pahrl an-glay

Where is the British consulate?
Où se trouve le consulat de Grande-Bretagne?
oo ser troov ler kon-sew-lah der grand-brer-tahn